# Nicole Kidman

Anatomy of an Actor

CAHIERS DU
CINEMA

# Nicole Kidman

Alexandre Tylski

| | Introduction | 6 |
|---|---|---|
| **1** | Rae Ingram<br>*Dead Calm* (1989)<br>Phillip Noyce | 18 |
| **2** | Suzanne Stone Maretto<br>*To Die For* (1995)<br>Gus Van Sant | 32 |
| **3** | Isabel Archer<br>*The Portrait of a Lady* (1996)<br>Jane Campion | 46 |
| **4** | Alice Harford<br>*Eyes Wide Shut* (1999)<br>Stanley Kubrick | 62 |
| **5** | Satine<br>*Moulin Rouge!* (2001)<br>Baz Luhrmann | 78 |
| **6** | Grace Stewart<br>*The Others* (2001)<br>Alejandro Amenábar | 94 |
| **7** | Virginia Woolf<br>*The Hours* (2002)<br>Stephen Daldry | 108 |
| **8** | Grace Margaret Mulligan<br>*Dogville* (2003)<br>Lars von Trier | 122 |
| **9** | Becca Corbett<br>*Rabbit Hole* (2010)<br>John Cameron Mitchell | 138 |
| **10** | Grace Kelly<br>*Grace of Monaco* (2014)<br>Olivier Dahan | 154 |
| | Conclusion | 171 |
| | Chronology | 174 |
| | Filmography | 178 |
| | Bibliography | 185 |
| | Notes | 186 |
| | Index | 190 |

# Introduction

A deceptively angelic blonde who favours charismatic filmmakers, epic sagas and dissimulating roles, Nicole Kidman works on films in a multitude of genres and with directors of different nationalities. Yet a common thread runs through her work, which is constantly re-energized by the same lifeblood: duplicity as a means of survival in the face of violence and death – like that practised by Scheherazade. Kidman has often played manipulators, enchantresses, courtesans, interpreters, artists, adventurers and other women threatened, bereaved and forced to dissimulate in order to survive. She is synonymous with desire, not only because she is perceived as a fatal beauty but above all because she herself, in her career, has repeatedly shown a desire for emancipation, exposure, risk-taking, regeneration and commitment. Essentially, not having been shaped by dogmas, but having drawn much inspiration from scriptwriters and filmmakers – from George Miller to Jane Campion and from Stanley Kubrick to Lars von Trier, by way of Gus Van Sant, Baz Luhrmann, Alejandro Amenábar and Werner Herzog – the independent Nicole Kidman is an existential artist.

## A Child of the '70s and a Teenager of the '80s

Nicole Mary Kidman – or 'Nicci', as her family nicknamed her – was born in Honolulu (Hawaii) in 1967. Her parents, Antony (who died in 2014) and Janelle, were, respectively, a psychologist and nurse. They lived for a time in Washington – where they demonstrated against the Vietnam War – then returned to Australia after the birth of Antonia, Nicole's younger sister. By the age of five, Nicci was already saying that she wanted to become an actress, but nobody yet took her seriously. Raised in a cultured family atmosphere, she grew up at a time when Australia was opening up to multiculturalism, which instilled values of tolerance in the future actress. Her memories explain the choices she would make as an actress: 'I was writing as a child. I couldn't understand why my mind was so dark. I had a strange relationship with death. I was captivated by the idea. I kept diaries, a journal. I put curses on the covers of the books to scare people away. I burned most of them just before I got married.

I'm very open to mystery... I think my darkness came from the capacity to love. I felt I had too much love to give. I was struck by the desire to live and the fear of it all being taken away.'[1]

The budding artist was very soon singing in a band, writing short stories (a secret garden she still cultivates) and taking dance and drama classes. At 16 she auditioned for a film student who wanted her to act in a short film but, due to shyness, she finally turned down the role. The director, then unknown, was Jane Campion, who wrote to the teenager, 'I hope one day we will work together. Be careful what you do, because you have real potential.'[2] Kidman went on to study drama at the Victorian College of the Arts in Melbourne, then at the Phillip Street Theatre and the Australian Theatre for Young People in Sydney – demanding schools where she was spotted by several directors, including John Duigan, who filmed her in *Flirting* (1991).

As a young woman, Kidman was set apart from her peers by her height (5ft 10in) and, more importantly, by the fact that she had a mother who was 'a feminist in a very conservative neighbourhood of Sydney, while her father... held left-wing views. She was Catholic while most of her friends were Protestant. Finally, her translucent skin, very sensitive to sunlight, obliged her to stay in her room and read. She saw this isolation as a curse, but has since realized that it was her chance. "I immersed myself in reading. And you don't read *Middlemarch* by George Eliot or *War and Peace* by Tolstoy and remain unchanged. I don't believe that anyone could identify more than me with the character of Natasha."'[3] Her passion for books has never left her; indeed, most of her films are literary adaptations.

The apprentice actress landed several television roles but interrupted her career to care for her mother, who was suffering from breast cancer. It was no doubt this experience that led to her later commitment to, among other causes, the United Nations Development Fund for Women (UNIFEM), the National Breast Cancer Foundation and the Stanford Women's Cancer Center. Once her mother had recovered, the young woman took part in the audio-visual revival that was taking place in Australia at the time, albeit in series and films that would now be considered

dated, including *BMX Bandits* (Brian Trenchard-Smith, 1983), and her first role for the cinema, *Bush Christmas* (Henri Safran, 1983). Kidman gradually gained experience and influence, landing some major roles, in particular that of the young activist Megan Goddard in the TV series *Vietnam* (Chris Noonan and John Duigan, 1987), which was a great success with both viewers and critics in Australia. She began to make a name for herself, thanks to her radiant face and natural maturity. The film *Emerald City* (Michael Jenkins, 1988) earned her the Best Supporting Actress award from the Australian Film Institute. At the end of the 1980s videos and home movies were taking television by storm and special-effect films, video games and Walkmans prevailed, while, in Australia, Kylie Minogue was a creating a hit with the TV series *Neighbours*. Nicole Kidman was ready to take flight.

---

The Gift of being Everywhere at Once

Although she left Australia in the early 1990s, Kidman remains, for film lovers the world over, the principal ambassadress for her country, well ahead of Cate Blanchett or Naomi Watts. Only Mel Gibson, at the height of his fame, could boast of giving such visibility to this far-off country. Some commentators, such as Pam Cook, have even alluded to Kidman in postcolonialist terms:

'During her Australian period, the formative years of her persona, Kidman's roles for television and film were independent heroines who were depicted in naturalistic mode tailored to character. These roles were in line with her public persona, which was based on principles of resilience, industriousness, determination and modernity underpinning white European Australian postcolonial ideals.'[4] Kidman still plays on that identity. In recent years she has returned to make films in her homeland or for Australian directors, reaffirming her relevance as an island-born, wild actress, whose influence extends well beyond the borders of Hollywood. Nevertheless, she has – and it is this that gives her such complexity – a particularly marked multicultural dimension.

Throughout her career Kidman has chosen to involve herself in productions that have forced her out of her comfort zone, in Ireland (*Far and Away* by Ron Howard in 1992), in Canada (*The Human Stain* by Robert Benton in 2003), in Slovakia (*The Peacemaker* by Mimi Leder in 1997), in Romania (*Cold Mountain* by Anthony Minghella in 2003) and in Morocco and Jordan (*Queen of the Desert* by Werner Herzog in 2015). Even when she works in the US, she does not necessarily favour New York or Los Angeles – indeed, she has chosen to live on a ranch in the wilds of Tennessee – willingly taking up roles in the state of Washington (*Practical Magic* by Griffin Dunne in 1998),

Above: Nicole Kidman in *Flirting* (1991) by John Duigan and *Bush Christmas* (1983) by Henri Safran.

Opposite: In *The Human Stain* (2003) by Robert Benton, Kidman plays Faunia Farley, a traumatized woman.

Following pages: Playing an unstable mother in *Stoker* (2013) by Park Chan-wook.

Louisiana (*Trespass* by Joel Schumacher in 2011, *The Paperboy* by Lee Daniels in 2012) or Tennessee (*Stoker* by Park Chan-wook, 2013).

Kidman is associated with both heat and cold, and sometimes of the most extreme variety (deserts, ice fields). Her type of environment is equally mixed, between urban and rural. The actress seems single-handedly to embody the words that Paul Auster rediscovered one day in a childhood notebook: 'The world is in my head, my body is in the world.'[5] The world is her stage, not in the sense of globalization, but in her compulsion to explore all facets of the planet, making this like a role in itself.

This gift of being everywhere at once, which is characterized by an obvious curiosity for other cultures, distinguishes her from many other contemporary actresses. Nevertheless, she is as much a professional as any of them, ready to appear as often as necessary to promote a film or cause. Kidman is not reluctant to take part in major American television programmes and talk shows and she can also be seen in the occasional documentary, including *Women on Top: Hollywood and Power* (Blake West, 2003) and *In Vogue: The Editor's Eye* (Fenton Bailey and Randy Barbato, 2012). She also lent her voice to *I Have Never Forgotten You: The Life & Legacy of Simon Wiesenthal* (Richard Trank, 2007). Essentially, all these commitments have made her a commodity star,[6] even though this function has been hijacked and distorted more than once during her career.

A Demanding Artistic Approach

An actor's skill is also gauged through the eyes of his or her partners and collaborators. Kidman has worked with a host of male and female actors of different nationalities and generations, and with very varied performing styles, although she has filmed several times with the same men: Tom Cruise, Stellan Skarsgård, Ed Harris, Christopher Walken, Daniel Craig, Colin Firth. By comparison, the list of women with whom Kidman has shared the billing, sometimes at her request, includes fewer stars but is no less important for that. She has worked twice with both Dianne Wiest (*Practical Magic* and *Rabbit Hole*) and Lauren Bacall (*Dogville* and *Birth*), two actresses she admires. To all these names we can add repeated working relationships with cinematographer Harris Savides and costume designer Ann Roth, both of whom have contributed significantly not only to the image we have of Kidman but also to the way in which she herself has constructed her image and, above all, has grasped a role, scene, expression or gesture. The collaboration between actors and these artists who work behind the scenes, who we too quickly refer to as technicians, ought to carry more weight in studies of actors.

Kidman, who has often played childless women, has also directed her attention towards violent roles regarding childhood, such as here, in *Birth* (2004) by Jonathan Glazer.

Following pages: Nicole Kidman and Tom Cruise, at that time her husband, on the set of *Far and Away* (1992) by Ron Howard.

As we know, in terms of directors, many great names have influenced Kidman's career. Other than those mentioned above, let us not forget Sydney Pollack (*The Interpreter*, 2005) and Philip Kaufman (*Hemingway & Gellhorn*, 2012). But neither should we neglect her need to work just as often with filmmakers who happen to be in a minority in the Hollywood industry, whether they are women (Jane Campion, Mimi Leder, Nora Ephron, Kim Farrant), openly gay (Gus Van Sant, Joel Schumacher, Rob Marshall, John Cameron Mitchell, Lee Daniels) or non-American, such as German Oliver Hirschbiegel (*The Invasion*, 2007), Australian Jonathan Teplitzky (*The Railway Man*, 2013) or British Rowan Joffé (*Before I Go to Sleep*, 2014). Neither does the actress hesitate in regularly giving filmmakers with little or no experience their chance: Jonathan Glazer (*Birth*, 2004), Steven Shainberg (*Fur: An Imaginary Portrait of Diane Arbus*, 2006), Paul King (*Paddington*, 2014) and Kim Farrant (*Strangerland*, 2015).

If one were to trace a common link between all these artists it would no doubt be the trust that Kidman has in them, the pleasure of feeling, in making films with them, a hint of rebellion, but also of style, novelty, the unknown or even a space for expression (and for risk-taking). Indeed, Kidman has worked with so many directors, some of whom were unknown to the general public for their first or second films that these occasionally

passed unnoticed, such as the awkward but enjoyable *Birthday Girl* (Jez Butterworth, 2001), which is at an intersection of genres – detective comedy, thriller and romantic comedy – and for which Kidman (Nadia) adopted a Russian accent and worked on her body language.

For all these reasons, so full is Kidman's filmography of intriguing characters and directors it was almost impossible to choose ten key films to present in this book. Yet we feel compelled to return to these particular roles: Kidman's first international début in *Dead Calm* (Phillip Noyce, 1989), her emergence as an actress of excellence in *To Die For* (Gus Van Sant, 1995), the complexities of her part in *The Portrait of a Lady* (Jane Campion, 1996), the revelations as she lifts the veil on her fantasies in *Eyes Wide Shut* (Stanley Kubrick, 1999), her ambivalent courtesan in *Moulin Rouge!* (Baz Luhrmann, 2001), the fanciful wanderings of her Grace Stewart in *The Others* (Alejandro Amenábar, 2001), her portrayal of Virginia Woolf in *The Hours* (Stephen Daldry, 2002), her character's intrusion in the community of *Dogville* (Lars von Trier, 2003), her depiction of grieving in *Rabbit Hole* (John Cameron Mitchell, 2010) and her celebrity actress–princess of *Grace of Monaco* (Olivier Dahan, 2014).

Little accustomed to worldwide commercial triumphs (although her films have grossed $2 billion – twice that of those of her compatriot

13

In *The Railway Man* (2014) by Jonathan Teplitzky, Nicole plays Patti Lomax, the wife of a British former POW during the Second World War.

In *Birthday Girl* (2001) by Jez Butterworth, she adopts a Russian accent to portray the character of Nadia.

Naomi Watts, though only half that of Julia Roberts, for example), Kidman, less timorous than other actresses of her generation, summarizes her choices very clearly: 'Most of my films have had mixed critical reviews. I don't choose middle-of-the-road directors. Some appeal to the majority, others a minority, but that suits me …'[7] Yet, behind all this composure and simplicity, she has created a body of work that is truly complex and highly textual, via the rocky road of a filmography that she is constantly questioning and redefining. She admits, 'I find filmmaking emotionally exhausting. It has saved me, but still, it's like a boxing match. You take blows. You can fall.'[8]

A Thousand and One Actresses in One

The birth of the legend that is Kidman came about thanks to the films (and personality) of Katharine Hepburn, which led Kidman to choose this career: 'I loved her free spirit, her refusal to conform, her fierce determination, her passion, her loyalty to herself, her inner fire.'[9] But this possible connection between these two particular actresses is not the only one imaginable – we could also consider Kidman's face in the light of that of Greta Garbo or Audrey Hepburn. For Roland Barthes, 'Garbo still belongs to that time in the cinema when the capture of the human face threw the crowds into disarray… Today, we are at the other end of this evolutionary spectrum: Audrey Hepburn's face, for example, is individualized not only by its distinctive themes (woman–child, woman–cat), but also by her person, by the almost unique specification of her face, which has nothing essential but consists of an infinite complexity of morphological functions. Like language, Garbo's uniqueness was conceptual; Audrey Hepburn's was substantial. Garbo's face is Idea, Hepburn's is Happening.'[10]

Within this context it is legitimate to perceive Kidman's face as a new step in female film faces, which can be defined as plural and existentialist. There has been no film, in fact, in which this face has not yet again changed its expression, meaning and incarnation, and even its tone, features, texture and structure. An actress devoid of personal mannerisms, fixed expressions and repetitive gestures (unlike Meryl Streep, for example), Kidman is continually transforming herself, never restricting her face or her body to particular habits or movements. Stéphane Bouquet and Jean-Marc Lalanne observe: 'Few actresses have reflected to this extent on the female identity as pure fabulous construction (robot, witch, ghost), monstrous in its obsession to comply with a norm, then, when it explodes out of this norm, with the limits of criminality and madness.'[11] More chameleon-like than most

legendary actresses that have preceded her, Kidman is indeed a surprise, a permanent work in progress, as though made of clay, a golem ceaselessly redefined, reinvented, depending on the film's period, subject, context and commitment.

In 2010, George Miller attempted to summarize the fascination her contemporaries have had for Kidman from very early on. At a reception organized by the American Cinematheque, the director compiled, on stage, keywords to define the actress whose career he had helped launch: 'Athletic', 'Born to be an actress', 'Talented', 'Rigorous', 'Ambitious', 'Excellence', 'Risk-Taker', 'Glamourous', 'Substantial', 'Courageous', 'Paradoxical', 'Child', 'Astute', 'Slim', 'Eager'. His lexicon, which was deliberately contradictory, contained dozens of words. It seems that Kidman is a continual paradox whose mystery might be self-perpetuating – as in the words of Michel Serres: 'all the statues are in fact black boxes whose secret partitions conceal someone or something they are hiding and protecting'.[12] A multifaceted performer, the epitome of the duplicity that lies at the heart of acting, Kidman has bewitched us from her very first films. And, in particular, with the first film of her international career, the superbly ironically titled *Dead Calm*.

Once upon a time there was Nicole Kidman.

# 1

# Rae Ingram

*Dead Calm* (1989)
Phillip Noyce

'In my heart I'm independent, a bit of a rebel, a non-conformist... I do characters that seem to be suffering from grief or dealing with grief or loss. And that probably is the kind of balance to extraordinary love... I am looking for things that take me out of my comfort zone.'[13]
Nicole Kidman, 2013

We are several minutes into the film before we see Nicole Kidman appear in her first major film role. Like John Ingram (Sam Neill), who is waiting for his wife Rae (Kidman) to come off the train, at first we are impatient, then we become anxious. The reunion of the model wife and her officer husband does not take place. We eventually find her, disfigured, confined to a hospital bed: she has been the victim of a car crash, which has taken the life of her young son. This is how viewers first encounter the woman who is to become one of the most glamorous film stars in the history of cinema, who is also one of the actresses who most likes to court danger, both physically and artistically.

In the Footsteps of Orson Welles

The film that launched Kidman's American career is pretty representative of her later choices. The synopsis alone reflects this: after the death of their child, Rae and John take to the sea in an attempt to recover from their loss, but a castaway, Hughie (Billy Zane), takes possession of the yacht when John goes off to inspect the one Hughie's escaped from. Rae is thus forced to cohabit with this disturbing young man. Meanwhile, John tries to survive, alone at sea, on a boat that is taking in water on all sides.

Shot off the coast of Queensland and with a cast of just three characters, *Dead Calm* is a claustrophobic thriller freely adapted from the eponymous novel by Charles Williams, published in 1963. This crime-fiction author saw his books adapted for the screen by some of the greatest directors, from Marcel Ophuls (*Banana Peel*, 1963) and Claude Sautet (*The Dictator's Guns*, 1965) to François Truffaut (*Confidentially Yours*, 1983) and Dennis Hopper (*The Hot Spot*, 1990). Before Phillip Noyce brought *Dead Calm* to the screen, Orson Welles had already shot an unfinished version in the 1960s, entitled *The Deep*, starring Jeanne Moreau, Oja Kodar, Laurence Harvey and the director himself. Only a few fragments of the film still exist.[14]

Essentially, one could say that Kidman's international career arose from this rather tragic incompletion, the work of a defeated genius so good at filming women. Doubtless, this visionary would have relished enhancing her from every possible angle and with every conceivable type of lighting. It was, in any case, Oja Kodar, Welles's former girlfriend, who gave the producer George Miller permission to make a new screen adaptation of the novel, for which she held the film rights. In exchange, the production team of *Dead Calm* agreed not to make a vulgar commercial film but rather to honour the poetry and freedom valued by Welles. Kodar also took this opportunity to get her revenge, choosing the ambitious Australian film industry over old Hollywood, whom she accused of having destroyed her lover.

In keeping with this spirit, the film's scriptwriter, Terry Hayes (author of the *Mad Max* franchise and the TV series *Vietnam*), praised the merits of Kidman – who had made an impression on him in *Vietnam* – to the film's producers. He even proposed rewriting the screenplay especially for her. Rae would no longer be a mature thirty-something woman but a young girl married to an older man. In fact, several established stars – notably Sigourney Weaver, who was used to physical roles – had already been approached for the role. Kidman, unknown outside her native country, was at that time only 19 years old. But her freshness, combined with her maturity, convinced Noyce and Miller. And, in fact, the age gap (20 years) between Sam Neill and the young woman does not really make itself felt. The actress's height (5 ft 10.5 in) and the youthful appearance of the New Zealand actor play their part in this. Surprisingly, there seems to be a bigger gap between Kidman and the American Billy Zane (despite the fact that they are only a year apart in age), which immediately reveals a striking contrast between the two actors.

Collaborating and Taking Risks

In 1987, despite the pressure of playing her first role in a big-budget feature film ($10 million,

In *Dead Calm*, audiences discovered a young actress who enjoys taking risks, both physically and artistically.

an enormous sum for an Australian film at that time), because she was surrounded by familiar and trusted faces, Kidman felt at ease. The shoot was, however, by no means a restful experience. Noyce very soon recalled the difficulties of filming at sea experienced by Roman Polanski during the making of *Knife in the Water* (1963) and *Pirates* (1986) and by Steven Spielberg for *Jaws* (1975). Some shots in *Dead Calm* took a whole day, others even two. One of the director's main intentions was to film the ocean as a lifeless, static place, in order to create tension. He also wanted to arouse a sense of constant anticipation in the audience, with very few action scenes. The use of Panavision enabled him to further isolate the actors within the setting, underlining their profound solitude to an even greater extent.

Fortunately, the 14 weeks of shooting went comparatively well, and Kidman proved daily that the producers had been right to take a chance in casting her. Whether sailing among the coral reef or acting in the studio (for the scenes below deck), she showed herself more than up to the challenge, insisting, for example, on learning how to manoeuvre the huge boat, even in high winds, as we see toward the end of the film. And so she got to grips with the main backdrop of the story, handling winches, cranks, shrouds and rudder with precision, and hoisting the sails with a dexterity worthy of a professional sailor. As she declared some years later, 'I try never to be governed by fear; that's how I choose things. If I ever feel that this is dangerous or I'm scared of it, then that probably draws me more towards it.'[15] She even played the film's violent and sex scenes herself, as she would continue to do unfailingly in the future: 'This is who I am as an actress: I don't want to turn things down because of my inhibitions or any self-censorship. I want to remain honest and true to the story and the character.'[16] In short, nothing fazes her and she does whatever it takes to portray her characters. The result for *Dead Calm* is that Rae lacks neither courage nor credibility.

## A New Face in Cinema

It is as though the strength of character and the light that emanate from Kidman directly expose the film. The striking aesthetic set up at the beginning of the movie, when we see a succession of white surfaces (the train, the naval caps and the lights in the hospital) leading to the close-up of the heroine's pupil as she lies on her sick bed, is pushed to its limits in the boat's pristine hull and the outfits chosen by the young bereaved mother. The film crew of *Dead Calm* clearly sensed that with this budding actress something special was happening before them: Kidman's pale skin, so sensitive to the sun, emits an incomparable luminosity that affirms the distinction between a young lead in a TV series and an extraordinary

star about to burst into the limelight. Critics sometimes differentiate between the 'presence' and the 'performance' of an actor: Kidman seems here to have already combined these two qualities.[17] She effortlessly marks *Dead Calm* with her aura, in her silences, through her movements and with a face that is new to the movie industry.

If the scriptwriter was inspired by her physical presence when writing the character of Rae, Kidman's face also determined choices made by the cinematographer, Dean Semler, who soon after won an Oscar for his work on *Dances with Wolves* (Kevin Costner, 1990). Her blue eyes, which tend toward emerald green in certain lights, reflect the nuances of the Pacific Ocean, in turn melancholy, frightened, suspicious, concentrated and determined. Whether seen looking up at the sky or in the dark, her pupils reflect the lens, reverse the focal distance, transfix the screen, respond to the horizon and blow us away. Of course, the cinema has immortalized many eyes: the resolute gaze of Katharine Hepburn, the timid and wild eyes of Lauren Bacall and the oblique regard of Hitchcock's heroines. It is as though, in *Dead Calm*, Kidman condenses and reinvents some of this established cinematic mode of expression.

## An Ophelian Interpretation

Disheveled hair, reddened cheeks and frightened cries: Rae awakens from sleep and sits up in bed. This is the first sequence of the film after the flashback showing the hospital and the car crash. The image portrayed by Kidman here is one of a return to reality, her features ravaged by a nightmare or by trauma. What if the earlier accident were only a bad dream? The anxiety disseminated since the beginning of the film leaves the way clear for different interpretations. For Marie Lherault, the grief caused by the child's death is not the predominant mood here: 'Through the grief and anxiety, it is above all Nicole's still-youthful sensuality that is exploited…, as though motherhood and sensuality were incompatible and [her sex appeal] could reach its climax only in fear.'[18] In any event, her suffocating, tangible terror makes a lie of the film's very title: nothing will be neither tranquil nor boring, despite appearances. No surface will be left peaceful, despite the silence and the absence of waves.

After this rude awakening, Rae dives into the sea, this time wearing black, into water that appears to be restorative and purifying. A flicker of a smile crosses her face. Filmed as a high-angle shot, with no horizon and without perspectives, the scene seems to promise a new calm. This pure water is seen as a cathartic liquid, a life-saving bath. The same scene will be reproduced at the end of the film, after the antagonist has disappeared. Rae's newfound inner peace

While filming at sea, Nicole Kidman insisted on learning how to handle, even in high winds, the huge sailboat that is the main backdrop of the story.

Following pages: Rae (Nicole Kidman) and her husband, John Ingram (Sam Neill). The age difference between the two actors (twenty years) is not readily apparent.

is represented by the new palette of colours: a rosy glow is now reflected in her face, and will remain there. This is no chance moment: before the beginning of the shoot, Noyce had asked Kidman to dye her hair, which is significant in terms of both the creation of the character and the aesthetics of the film. Rae's red hair merges with the mahogany of the boat, the sunsets, the distress flares and the blood. In short, the world is engulfed in her hair, and she becomes all-encompassing, a deity in the image of Botticelli's Venus, posed on her shell, overlooking the vastness of the ocean.

Combined with Kidman's captivating grace, this supposedly anodyne bathing scene produces the desired effect. The moment might have been inspired by a verse from Rimbaud's *Ophelia* (1870), which we will rediscover in *The Hours* (2002): 'On billows calm and black where the stars are sleeping / The white Ophelia floats like a giant lily / Floats ever so slowly, resting in her long veils… For more than a thousand years mournful Ophelia / White ghost, has passed over the long black river.'[19] On closer inspection, *Dead Calm* 'Opheliarizes' the Pacific Ocean, which is portrayed in this moment, in its exceptional calm, as stagnant and therefore deadly. Rae (a name of Hebrew origin, meaning 'ewe') is perhaps Ophelia carried by the current before attempting a return to life. Whether as siren or muse, mermaid or nymph, Rae makes the ocean the scene of her grieving process. Her bathing becomes a renaissance that prepares her to find the necessary strength to fight the monster that is about to appear. Our first view of him is his back, while he is rowing so frantically that he hits into the hull of the couple's stylish schooner.

*Dead Calm* is also witness to a transformation that is underway as Kidman learns to harness every inch of her body. In faking her attraction for Hughie she shows us how she is able to fulfil her role of the perfect actress. This initiation – the meticulous observation of a young woman who is emerging before us – is a thread that runs throughout the film. She manages to create a hybrid character: ethereal when she is on the bridge but a prisoner below deck; at ease in the open air or in the water but doomed to suffocate, like a bird in a gilded cage and dehumanized like a lost sheep ready to be sacrificed. Rae is probably less woman–child than genuine child, curled up and uncertain, on the point of becoming a woman, giving birth to her own identity as the adventure progresses. She learns to use the harpoon and steers the boat herself, less like a figurehead than a female privateer of the sort that existed in the nineteenth century.

Compared to Rae, Hughie symbolizes the wolf – a sort of Brando, muscled like a Greek god, a raging, sweating madman, opening his mouth wide as though to devour her, notably when he seizes a firearm. Fortunately, the elements unleash their fury at the opportune moment, and Rae, who has quickly got the measure of her enemy and his capacity for unchecked rage, has managed to get him to drink a timely cocktail of sedatives. 'We were friends,' howls Hughie, a caged beast who tries to strangle her. For it is a question of taming the madness of this psychopath whose monstrosity we have already witnessed as we follow John's macabre discoveries. After she has threatened and shot him with the crossbow, wounding him, Hughie grins. Rae's calm and resignation reveals a new face: that of a woman who is in control in even the most extreme situations. Yet, setting up a nice paradox, Hughie has declared his love for her: 'You know I was watching you when you were sleeping. And I've got to tell you that your face fascinates me. Yeah, even when you're eighty Rae, you'll still be a beautiful woman […] You've got magnificent bone structure.' As Lherault writes, 'the scene of the rape consented to by Rae in order to escape from her abductor offers the audience the spectacle of the actress's naked body. While we never see Rae and John making love in the film, this scene allows the director to spotlight a woman bearing an enigmatic expression – something between pleasure, manipulation and terror – that will reappear often in her career.'[20] It is also Kidman's total abandonment that enthrals us in these images, the young woman using every part of her body, as one would to raise an army, in order to overcome her natural shyness. This is the leitmotif that recurs in her subsequent choices of roles: getting as close as possible to fear and the enemy in order to dominate them.

John, on the other hand, is a man of few words, who communicates literally in Morse code during a large part of the film, giving rise to some great scenes where Rae talks and cries into the void, not knowing whether he can hear her. Even if she manages to get the boat's radio to work, she is literally powerless in front of it, and she herself becomes speechless and lost. Kidman would have to portray such solitude in front of the camera in numerous films: it seems that directors particularly appreciate this aspect of her performance. Desperately alone in this scene and this image, Kidman plays using her own emotions, but always with restraint, as if she is in suspension – as can be observed in her lips, which are often slightly apart. We do not know what most terrorizes her here: losing contact with her husband or forced cohabitation with Hughie. As Pam Cook points out, 'Kidman's body language, movements and facial expressions are economically geared to rendering Rae's gradual understanding of how dangerous Hughie is. She makes no unnecessary gestures, and throughout the film her relationship to objects is utilitarian, limited to their narrative function.'[21]

For Rae, John is both Ulysses and Orpheus: he symbolically abandons his wife before saving her

Although she began her career in an Australian TV drama series in the 1980s, Kidman did not feel particularly inclined to return to television once her film career had launched. However, over the years, in addition to guest appearances on TV programmes, the actress has often involved herself in television projects, for example the glamorous *Somethin' Stupid*, music video that was broadcast repeatedly on channels worldwide in 2001, in which she sang with Robbie Williams.

Kidman's finest/most notable television appearance to date, however, is *Hemingway & Gellhorn*, the lavish 2012 TV movie (which had a budget of $14 million) directed by Philip Kaufman and produced by HBO. Excited by the role of Martha Gellhorn, the famous journalist and third wife of Hemingway (played by Clive Owen), she said, 'I watched lots of documentaries in which she appeared; I listened to old interviews she'd given. I slightly changed her accent, which was very British in her youth. My voice needed to be darker because she smoked a lot. She was a woman with incredible strength of character. I had access to her writings, so to her innermost being. She was the first female war correspondent and decided to join the boys' club. Like all women, she was expected to make compromises, to conform to society's norms. Martha Gellhorn refused to do so; she wanted to follow her own desires, her own heart. She refused, in her marriage, to be submissive and domesticated.'[a]

Barely halfway through her career, Kidman is thus not only an important face in world cinema, but has also been a figure in television for more than three decades. And the best, it would seem, is yet to come.

from hell (*Orpheus* is also the name of the boat he tries to refloat). When Rae grabs his hand and saves his life at the end of the film, the story might have ended there and left the triumph of rescue with the heroine. Yet the ending is just the opposite, despite the fact that Rae managed to find herself, then go back and save her husband. In this respect, it is possible to regard the epilogue as a return to the patriarchal order: John returns to the helm of the boat, Rae becomes a mermaid again and John kills the young pretender. This ending would perhaps never have seen the light of day had the film been shot a few years later, once Kidman had become a star. This final scene had been requested by the distributor Warner, with the agreement of the scriptwriter (who was unhappy with his initial idea), following a test screening where the audience clearly wanted Hughie dead. Did Hollywood finally get the better of a project that was meant to be independent, open-ended and Wellesian? What would a current audience think of this rather macho finale, now that we expect so much of Kidman as a strong female figure?

## At the Crossroads

In the final analysis, even during the making of her first major film Kidman was already having an influence on its scriptwriter, filmmaker and cinematographer. More importantly, she was beginning to form her creative vision, by expressing her interest, notably, in portraits of women in danger or obliged to play a particular role in order to survive. Kidman, who would later play another traumatized heroine in *The Human Stain* (2003) by Robert Benton, explains: 'I have always tried to be a woman who protects other women. I have a sister, I have daughters, I have girlfriends, and I was raised by a feminist mother. Being a feminist doesn't mean that you hate men, it just means that we need to protect and help each other. I want women to know I am on their side, because sometimes being a woman is tough, and sometimes there is more criticism of what we do. We are judged more harshly than men, and that is why camaraderie is important.'[22]

*Dead Calm* was released in cinemas in spring 1989, at the crossroads between two eras. It heralded a wave of films about serial killers, most likely in reaction to a globally rather bland decade. But this release also coincided with others in which several women made impressions in strong roles: Sigourney Weaver in *Gorillas in the Mist* by Michael Apted, Melanie Griffith in *Working Girl* by Mike Nichols, Jodie Foster in *The Accused* by Jonathan Kaplan, Glenn Close in *Dangerous Liaisons* by Stephen Frears, and Meryl Streep in *A Cry in the Dark* by Fred Schepisi. In this unusual context, criticism was generally favourable – despite fault frequently being found with the conclusion – and critics were

Opposite: Clive Owen (Ernest Hemingway) and Nicole Kidman (Martha Gellhorn) in the TV movie *Hemingway & Gellhorn* (2012) by Philip Kaufman.

Above: Rae must tame the madness of a psychopath whose monstrosity viewers have already witnessed.

excited by this newcomer, who from time to time overshadowed the performances of Neill and Zane, however successful they were. *Variety* paid tribute to the performance of the young actress who 'gives the character of Rae real tenacity and energy',[23] while the *Washington Post*, literally captivated, accorded Rae a place 'in the pantheon of heroines, an Amazon for the '90s'.[24] Over 15 years later, David Thomson observes that 'if Rae keeps her eyes open during the lovemaking, still she is not cold or numb to it. There is a sexual readiness in Kidman's presence [... It] would be a little more interesting if Rae had felt a twinge of sexual confusion and guilt. And I don't think it would be possible to think of that extra if Rae had been, say, a decent wife of the proper age. It is the fact that she is young, sexy and unresolved that gives the film its secret spark. And that is why Kidman got "noticed" in *Dead Calm*... There was a question mark in her needy eyes, and audiences as well as future filmmakers felt challenged to answer it.'[25] For Cook, Kidman was 'presented as a future international star and significant Australian export'.[26]

After *Dead Calm*, Kidman took part in the TV mini-series *Bangkok Hilton* (written for her by Hayes and produced by Miller), one of several series, including *Emerald City* and *Vietnam*, for which she won a string of awards in Australia. A chapter had ended. She then flew to New York to take on a role for Tony Scott in the action movie *Days of Thunder*, where she met her future husband, the superstar Tom Cruise. Thus began a toing and froing between personal projects and big-budget productions, with the added difficulty for Kidman of how to exist as 'the wife of' while redoubling her efforts to prove her worth as an artist no matter what.

# 2

# Suzanne Stone Maretto

*To Die For* (1995)
Gus Van Sant

'I'd had enough of playing makeweight to all those male stars of Hollywood. Now I'm going to tread on them.'[27]
Nicole Kidman, 1995

The Ambitious Nicole Kidman

*To Die For* arrived at just the right time for Kidman. Since *Days of Thunder* (Tony Scott, 1990), in which she played a doctor who veered more toward sexy nurse than health-care professional, her name had been linked with that of Tom Cruise, whom she had married in December 1990. In the world of Hollywood the young Australian was 'Mrs. Tom Cruise', an image that was reinforced by the other film they had made together, the conventional *Far and Away* (Ron Howard, 1992). The actress was settling for unambitious roles, playing characters whose existence is strictly determined by the men around her. For example, she was the charming asset of *Billy Bathgate* (Robert Benton, 1991), opposite Dustin Hoffman and Bruce Willis; the devoted wife of a man with terminal cancer, played by Michael Keaton in *My Life* (Bruce Joel Rubin, 1993); and a damsel in distress in *Batman Forever* (Joel Schumacher, 1995). It was difficult, in such conditions, to be recognized as an artist in her own right, even though her performance in *Billy Bathgate* had earned her a Golden Globe nomination for Best Supporting Actress. In fact, it would take a lot to satisfy Kidman's ambition: to be the star of a film, to work with an unconventional director, to break away from a bland image that risked paralysing her and to portray a role that meant something for her. Nearly 30 years old, she was already sufficiently well known and established in the star system to strike out. She just needed to find that rare pearl. This was to be *To Die For*.

Deciding to make her own luck, Kidman managed to get hold of Gus Van Sant's private phone number and called him, at home, to persuade him to engage her for his new film, an adaption of the book by Joyce Maynard. She was convinced, in fact, that she knew how to portray the young woman who had inspired the novel. (In 1990, a New Hampshire regional news employee, Pamela Smart, had coerced her 15-year-old lover, for love of her, into killing her husband. Her trial, which made headlines, was the first to be broadcast in its entirety on American television.) In addition, the actress accepted a fee ($2 million dollars) that was half that offered to Meg Ryan, who had initially been lined up for the part. Jennifer Jason Leigh and Patricia Arquette had also been in the running for a while, but it was Kidman's determination that made the difference.

To prepare for the role, Kidman worked on disguising her Australian accent beneath Californian intonations and watched hours and hours of local TV programmes, particularly weather forecasts, to explore the many ways used by television presenters to 'flirt with the camera', something David Thomson highlights in his book about her.[28] The scriptwriter Buck Henry (the sarcastic and colourful writer of *The Graduate*, *Catch-22* and *Heaven Can Wait*) imagined a job as a weather presenter for Pamela Smart, who becomes Suzanne Stone, and makes the character an ambitious and narcissistic monster, obsessed with her own hype. When her husband, Larry Maretto (Matt Dillon), asks her to devote more time to her family, she decides to have him killed in order to eliminate, with no reservations, anything that might get in the way of her career.

The film crew of *To Die For*, who were initially sceptical about Kidman's ability to handle such a role, were quickly won over, in particular the film's producer, Laura Ziskin, who declared, 'When she came in, I realized "she knew" something about this part. It was her. That's when I learnt she's not an *ingénue*. She's a character actress in an *ingénue* package. We put a blonde wig on her curly red hair. It was a eureka moment. I thought, Carole Lombard! Once we started, she slayed us. It was brilliant and people were laughing on set.'[29] During the shoot she built up a real rapport with her other cast members, whether experienced actors, such as Dillon and Joaquin Phoenix (Jimmy, Suzanne's lover), or newcomers (Casey Affleck and Alison Folland, the teenagers fascinated by the young woman). Supported and encouraged, the actress felt at ease on set and was surrounded by a team who were often enchanted by her unexpected and caustic performance. This atmosphere enabled her to confidently elaborate the many tonal nuances of her character.

After several unambitious roles, Kidman wanted to be the star of a film, work with an unconventional director and break away from a bland image that risked paralysing her. Her meeting with Gus Van Sant was a defining moment.

## A Chilling Composition

When the film begins, in a small snow-covered town in the north of the United States, Suzanne Stone appears hidden behind dark glasses – those of an inconsolable widow, one would assume, as we see her at her husband's funeral. And yet she looks more like a star hounded by the press than a woman in mourning. The opening credits, which include press cuttings whose sensationalist headlines accompany cleverly composed photographs of Suzanne, set the tone.[30] Everything will be about appearances. In fact, Suzanne exists only through the media coverage of her image. The camera zooms in on an image of her face, enlarging it so that we see its pixelation. Her face cannot resist this meticulous observation and literally disappears, as though riddled with bullets, pierced, empty. The voice-over of the character makes it clear: to appreciate overall coherence, you need to know how to keep your distance. This voice, at first disembodied, also seems to warn us of the doublespeak to come. What the character will say will not necessarily correspond with how she appears, nor with reality.

When the voice at last comes together with the image, the young woman appears on the screen, dressed in a candy-pink outfit and gold-plated jewellery. Wearing mauve and pink make-up, she is filming an interview against a pristine white backdrop. Within the first few seconds, Kidman manages to portray a woman who is magnetized by the camera and by her own reflection. Her gaze is that of a machine, fixed, imperturbable, while she strings together a series of stereotyped pouts and stock phrases, articulated in a crooning voice. Her calibrated speech combines pauses and pedantic pronouncements, such as when she takes care to distinguish her married name – Suzanne Maretto, too middle-class and, most importantly, not 'a name you can remember' – from her 'professional' name. She particularly detaches this adjective, which alerts us, from the very beginning of the film, to the fact that Suzanne lives only for her career. We intuit, nevertheless, that her smile and self-assurance are too studied to be completely genuine. As Pam Cook notes, 'Kidman's portrayal of the monstrous Suzanne produces an ambivalent response in the viewer, who is caught between derision for the character and admiration for the execution of the role.'[31] It is hard to imagine Meg Ryan bringing to the role the same icy composure, the same absence of self-mockery that Kidman manages to convey. For what truly characterizes Suzanne is her absolute determination and total lack of introspection. Whether in relation to the man she has chosen for herself or the job she covets, Suzanne Stone 'knows only one way to get what she wants: to charge straight ahead, like a bulldozer, crushing without the slightest qualm any obstacle that finds

In the first meeting between Suzanne and her future husband, she plays with the straw in her glass (a recurring motif in the film) while gazing at him in an explicit way.

Opposite: Nicole Kidman with Casey Affleck, Joaquin Phoenix and Alison Folland during a break in filming.

Following pages: Suzanne plays the vamp for her husband, Larry Maretto (Matt Dillon).

itself between her and the object of her desire'.[32] So it is less by strategic means than by a process of tenacity that she manages to land a job as a weather presenter, mechanically persisting in her quest, as is suggested in the elliptical montage that runs together Suzanne's interventions with the station manager.

### Polymorphous and Monstrous

Suzanne's many outfits give her the appearance of a stereotypical 1950s woman: outrageous make-up (including spectacular lipstick), pert breasts and colours that are reminiscent of Douglas Sirk's films. In this respect, Kidman's love of fashion undoubtedly serves the film well, as she appears in a series of sometimes very short scenes wearing a different outfit in each (coordinated by Hungarian costume designer Beatrix Aruna Pasztor). These successive outfits could almost be compared to a Warhol experiment, in the style of his reproductions of Marilyn Monroe's face. Rarely will an actress change her skin so many times in the same film. Like a painter, Kidman discusses tones, textures and colours (sometimes in relation to the settings and wallpapers) and invariably adapts her pose according to the clothes she is wearing, because Suzanne knows exactly how to show herself to advantage and how to seduce. In the first meeting between the young woman and her future husband, an

amateur drummer in a rock band, she is dressed Lolita-style and plays with the straw in her glass (a recurring motif in the film) while gazing at him in an explicit way. While other groupies shimmy to the rhythms created by the young musician, Suzanne remains motionless, using only this little secret weapon to take him down. For here she is the incarnation of a 'showy and desirable vision of fully-fledged femininity'.[33] The fascination she later holds for the teenagers who participate in her documentary clearly shows her powers of seduction. But the perverse game she plays with them adds another dimension to the character, that of the pleasure of transgression: 'The simple satire about self-promotion… becomes the story of a desire that turns out to be polymorphous, the portrait of a many-tiered, complex clinical case, but one that is completely unaware of this complexity and is probably mistaken in what it wants.'[34] So, Suzanne is not content merely to arouse: she also inflames and manipulates the desire. Once she becomes aware of the need to kill her husband, she develops an aggressive strategy to rally the teenagers to her cause. Especially memorable is the sequence where she is trying on underwear in front of schoolgirl Lydia, or when she invites her and Jimmy, a classmate, to her house. In this sequence, Kidman creates one of the first occurrences of the 'sorceress', a recurring motif in her career. And this dimension is made explicit by the song used in the closing credits,

'Season of the Witch' (Donovan, 1966), which puts the finishing touches to this maleficent and ironic portrait. Playing a being half-woman, half-animal, wearing an angora sweater, the actress begins by stretching like a cat while waiting for the arrival of her prey. When she wiggles her fingers, her arms stretched out to Jimmy, Suzanne looks like a witch about to spellbind her lover. Stéphane Bouquet and Jean-Marc Lalanne also draw our attention to the reference to *Bell, Book and Candle* (Richard Quine, 1958) in the sequence where Larry's sister is complaining about Suzanne: on the television set behind her the modern-day witch played by Kim Novak removes her cat from James Stewart's shoulder.[35] When Suzanne gives her weather forecast at the moment her husband is to be executed, her eyes are wild, frightening. Her head, which leans forward slightly, makes her eyes seem even larger and transforms her into the Bride of Frankenstein. The shadows of Joan Crawford, Bette Davis and Barbara Stanwyck inevitably project themselves onto this composition. We are also reminded of Gloria Swanson at the end of *Sunset Boulevard* (Billy Wilder, 1950), when her character, over-the-hill ex-star Norma Desmond, poses for the television cameras after having assassinated her lover. A similar sequence shows Suzanne receiving attention from the press after the murder of her husband. Her whole body seems to tense and swell with inner ecstasy as she faces the bright lights of glory.

## Bovary and Kidman

The character of Suzanne evokes for some the figure of Madame Bovary, as noted by journalist and author Fabrice Pliskin: '[…] a modern bovarism where sitcoms and docudramas have replaced keepsakes. Like Emma, Suzanne is always overdressed, always hovering between the sublime and the ridiculous. Like Emma, she is too much. Too snobbish, too greedy. Like Emma, she wants objects less for their own sake than for the desire they excite in others.'[36] Everything is about appearance, and Suzanne's remarks sometimes border on the ridiculous, especially when Kidman avoids any suggestion of irony when uttering comments such as, 'I believe that Mr. Gorbachev – you know, the man who ran Russia for so long? – I believe that he would still be in power today if he'd done what so many people suggested and had that big purple thing taken off his forehead.' The character's stupidity and sincerity are disarming and this weakness allows the nuancing of this portrait of a greedy psychopath. When Suzanne decides to spend her honeymoon in Miami, the artificial and flashy paradise that so resembles her, she is actually going there for calculated careerist reasons, in order to secretly monitor the National Association of Broadcasters Conference and meet with media professionals.

Her discussion over a cocktail with the speaker of the day drives home to her that she will need to sleep with the right people if she wants to succeed in television, as have others before her. When the journalist starts stroking her leg, Kidman manages to convey both her character's discomfort and her compliance. Suzanne's gaze, until then perfectly fixed on the person speaking to her, changes direction several times. At the same time, the young woman tilts her head as if by reflex and puts her hand to her neck in a seductive pose. Unsure of herself, she ends up grasping the drinking straw in the cocktail he has ordered for her. Kidman is thus able to make us feel pity for her character, through her baffled naivety, her wide-open mouth and eyes, and her absence of professional status: she is nothing and she is being spoken to as if she is a nobody. Her dream of social elevation and obsession with the limelight are revealed as being synonymous with prostitution and humiliation. In addition, throughout this sequence, the lighting leaves her face in shadow, distorting her features in a frightening way, as if the behind-the-scenes ugliness of show business was backfiring on her, physically contaminating her. This episode marks a turning-point in Suzanne's resolve. Back in her small town, she will prove to be even more determined, more than ever ready to do anything, infected with the idea of success, even to the point of offering her body.

Kidman gives us a sometimes touching and always honest portrait of a strong-willed, passionate woman who longs, whatever the cost, to free herself from a narrow-minded community and the rather antiquated attitude of her husband. By playing devil's advocate, she manages, here and there, with subtle touches, to modulate the bitch that we want to see Suzanne Stone as. She depicts her as someone who wants to extricate herself from her status as a wife who is being asked to toe the line and become a mother as soon as possible. In a short scene, she even makes Suzanne yawn when faced with a bunch of noisy, excited children (whom she definitely does not want to have to deal with) and is able to make this young loose canon sympathetic.

## An Artist is Born

Augmented by Kidman's figure and grace, *To Die For* brought a colourful and feminine touch to a rather sombre period in cinema when films about male serial killers were at their height. Without placing Suzanne Stone in the same category as Hannibal Lecter, the actress's cynical performance is ultimately every bit as good as other portrayals of psychopaths in American movies of the 1990s. In fact, Kidman conveys more restraint, sophistication and reflection on show business and the role of women in this world. The film

was presented at the Cannes Film Festival in May 1995. During the press conference the actress did not hide her ambitions, even if they were still conditioned by the reputation of her famous husband: 'I want to exist in my own right, not simply as a reflection of Tom's glory. With Gus Van Sant's talent and acerbic tone, I knew that I could at last change my image and escape from all stereotypes. For this role, I spent my nights watching television. Until then, this world was unknown to me. So I stole everything from the screen! There's no shortage of malice in the world of television.'[37]

Kidman seduced the international press, both male and female. Thus we read in *Le Figaro* a description, almost bewitched, that perhaps suits her own persona as well as Suzanne Stone's, allying both control freak and fashion victim: 'Long curly hair, immaculate make-up and opalescent dress, Kidman takes everyone in with her doll-like charm. Behind her charming porcelain-like face with its innocently blue eyes hides a determined woman and an actress with nerves of steel… She signs film stills with an angelic smile, but is worried, after the signing, to see a photograph in circulation that has not had her approval. She sports with the same grace a chic Parisian black Chanel suit and a wild geranium, black and pink flamenco dress by John Galliano, complete with fan, chewing gum and discreet glasses.'[38]

The *Chicago Tribune* hailed 'a characterization of breathtakingly controlled artifice, dead-on timing, dizzyingly precise humor'.[39] For *Cahiers du cinéma*, her performance was also a thing of precision: 'Nicole Kidman knows how to make her every expression, vocal inflexion and gesture expressive, significant and necessary.'[40] But it was perhaps Pliskin, writing in *Le Nouvel Obs*, who defines her best: 'In *To Die For*, Nicole Kidman has the body of a giant, the body of a cathodic robot strapped into a prime-time mini-skirted suit, a body so impeccably sculpted for the small screen that it looks awkward, even comic, as soon as it leaves the television set to walk the streets of everyday life, like a sort of Hollywood albatross whose silicone wings prevent it from flying. […] Kidman reproduces the grammar of automatic eyebrows, which was rife at CNN until Claire Chazal's news reports, that consists of a gloomy knitting together of the brows when announcing a flood and a joyful raising of them, a second later, to talk about a ballet or the birth of a baby panda. Suzanne is *mediabolical*.' And she concludes, 'Mrs Tom Cruise destroys her bland image.'[41]

Nicole Kidman had succeeded. As Cook highlights, 'This period saw a transition from her Australian identity to a less specific version of modern womanhood. She began to adopt an American accent, her image became groomed and glamorised and her acting more stylised.'[42] The film thus enabled some commentators to see a

To successfully manage her career, Kidman has relied heavily on a plan that has worked well for other stars (including for Meryl Streep, for example), particularly during the 1970s: alternating personal films and commercial blockbusters. This regime enables the actress to maintain her visibility and commercial viability, while still upholding her artistic standards. Looking at her filmography, we not only see a cleverly orchestrated succession of weighty films with famous co-stars and directors partners, but also, over the years, a growing desire to be associated with art-house pictures made by key names. She made the action film *The Peacemaker* (Mimi Leder, 1997) just after a Henry James story for Jane Campion (*The Portrait of a Lady*, 1996), but her next roles saw her playing a Russian immigrant in the small British film *Birthday Girl* (Jez Butterworth, 2001) and a singer in the glitzy and ambitious *Moulin Rouge!*

(Baz Luhrmann, 2001). In 2003, she not only lit up Anthony Minghella's world, starring in his epic *Cold Mountain*, but also Lars von Trier's unusual, experimental set in *Dogville*. And between two film oddities – *Birth* (Jonathan Glazer, 2004) and *Fur: An Imaginary Portrait of Diane Arbus* (Steven Shainberg, 2006) – Kidman made two stylish Hollywood movies in 2005: *The Interpreter* by Sydney Pollack and *Bewitched* by Nora Ephron. In 2007, Kidman opened the Telluride Film Festival, itself a symbol of independent cinema, with *Margot at the Wedding* (Noah Baumbach) but also walked the red carpet of major premieres to promote *The Golden Compass* (Chris Weitz). Two huge productions (both costing around $100 million) followed: *Australia* (Baz Luhrmann, 2008) and *Nine* (Rob Marshall, 2009), before another small-budget film, *Rabbit Hole* (John Cameron Mitchell, 2010). Since then, the actress seems to have involved

herself in medium-weight films (with budgets between $10–30 million), such as the unrestrained *The Paperboy* (Lee Daniels, 2012), the psychological thriller *Stoker* (Park Chan-wook, 2013) and the more conventional *The Railway Man* (Jonathan Teplitzky, 2013). Has this balance led to a certain tepidity in her recent projects? Should she return to wider variations between projects and make fewer films? It is hard to say. In any case, if art is about staying the course, maintaining her position as a star with high standards will be a difficult tightrope walk.

Opposite: Nicole Kidman in *Birth* (2004) by Jonathan Glazer. She plays the role of a young widow whose husband seems to be reincarnated in a ten-year-old boy.

Suzanne Maretto and her young lover (Joaquin Phoenix), whom she has manipulated into doing away with her husband, who is a potential hindrance to her career plans.

subversion of the actress's image, hitherto considered sterile, while others saw in it a sort of putting to death of part of her identity. In any case, with this more Brechtian than Stanislavskian, more self-reflective than simply internalized, performance, she rewrote a new chapter in her career and revealed a new aspect of her talent.

Although the film met with only moderate commercial success in the US, *To Die For* won Kidman her first Golden Globe as Best Actress, a prestigious award from the international press. More than a star, an artist was born. Conscious of this new challenge and its inherent pressures, she maintained her course of artistic ambition by shooting her next film with the recent winner of the Palme d'Or (for *The Piano*, 1993), great film director and fellow Antipodean Jane Campion.

# 3

# Isabel Archer

*The Portrait of a Lady* (1996)
Jane Campion

'Isabel is in an emotionally abusive relationship and, as an actor, you have to use that; it's very intense and it's very upsetting. There's deep shame and humiliation, because you're being put through these things that are very hard to allow to happen to yourself.'[43]
Nicole Kidman, 1996

Kidman loves period films: 'I feel at ease in the past. My liking for the past comes, no doubt, from the literature I used to read avidly in my youth, whether Russian, English or French; writers like Thomas Mann and Proust.'[44] The chance to enter into the world of Henry James was an even more attractive proposition because of the connection she felt with the director, New Zealand-born Jane Campion, who said of her, 'Nicole has extraordinary potential: a lot of self-confidence and yet a lot of doubts at the same. She was the perfect choice for Isabel. Yet, at one stage during preparation, I became suddenly afraid that she wasn't the character and I asked her permission to shoot the rehearsals. That lasted for two days. Few stars would have complied with that sort of exercise.'[45] The actress portrays Isabel Archer, a romantic idealist who, despite her likeable suitors, wants to be loved by a man who is cold and proud, the darkly mysterious Gilbert Osmond (John Malkovich).

As is witnessed in *The Making of* video directed by Peter Long and Kate Ellis, shooting the film was both exhausting and exhilarating. Due to the psychological complexity of the relationships between the characters, each scene presented Kidman with a new emotional challenge. Sometimes she felt overwhelmed by the flood of feelings she had to deal with. Sometimes she would continue crying after the end of the takes. Campion would often go and comfort her but she also pushed Kidman to her limits, telling her, 'You can't pretend, you must feel what you're acting.'[46] The actress was troubled by uncertainties, wondering whether the audience and the critics would reproach her for crying too much, given the number of scenes where she is in tears. She also conceded that in addition to the emotional challenges of the role, the shoot was physically demanding: 'I've never had a film where I've had to do twenty-five takes over and over again, so you have to be able to constantly reproduce it. And particularly with the way she moves the camera a lot. As an actor you have to be emotionally present each time. Some days you come in and just don't wanna go here and I'd fight Jane on it and she'd say that you have to, and she'd really push me, times when it's just not there, I don't feel anything, I feel dead, I can't feel anything, and you get more and more agitated and everything kind of shuts down. "Breathe, breathe and relax" and it's there.'[47]

Shooting lasted fourteen weeks, in several countries, and her on screen partners, John Malkovich, Viggo Mortensen and Barbara Hershey, were all strong-willed. As Marie Lherault recalls, 'Nicole also carries the project as one carries a child…. To really get into the skin of this new character, Nicole made herself wear a corset: incidentally, she suffered several dizzy spells on the set. The actress even went down with a high fever at the end of the shoot, taking to her bed for two weeks.'[48] But this experience gave Kidman's performance, which is characterized by introspection and restraint, a new degree of power and precision.[49]

## An Ambiguous Role

The first image that follows the opening credits of *The Portrait of a Lady* is a close-up of Isabel's face. The young woman is emotionally stirred, tears in her eyes and breathing deeply – as though this were a final scene. Kidman seems to embody the psychology of the character and to perhaps, at the same time, refer forward to the contemporary women that Campion filmed for the opening credits. As in *To Die For*, the camera zooms in on her eyes, but here she is dressed in black, with no gaudy colours, no smile and no intention to be either ugly or beautiful, with her rather coarse mop of red hair. As the filmmaker explains, 'It was Nicole's idea to have this frizzy hairstyle, because she'd had hair like that as a child and didn't like herself like that. She most definitely didn't want her character to be a beauty.'[50]

Isabel is fuming. In the shade beneath the drooping branches of a tree, she looks like a frightened bird, alarmed by the arrival of a man, Lord Warburton (Richard E. Grant), of whom we see only his boots at first. She quickly dries her eyes and looks up at the man who has just

Despite her likeable suitors, Isabel Archer, a romantic idealist, wants to be loved by a man who is cold and proud, the darkly mysterious Gilbert Osmond (John Malkovich).

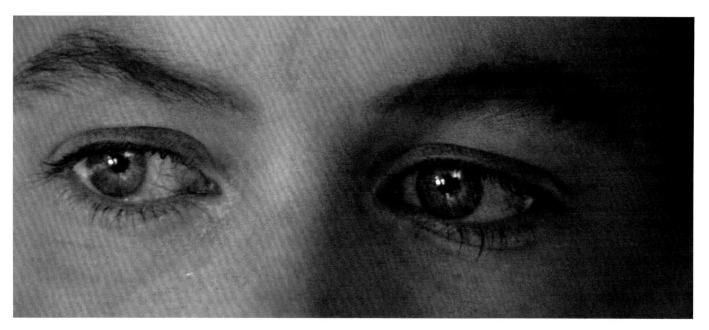

Opposite: Isabel, in tears. In the shade beneath the drooping branches of a tree, she looks up at the man who has just invaded her space, Lord Warburton (Richard E. Grant). The roles are then reversed: he kneels down to declare his love for her, and she gets up and leaves.

Above: Only a shadow of herself, Isabel frequently appears in silhouette. The *chiaroscuro* that surrounds her emphasizes this in-between state.

invaded her space. The roles are then reversed: he kneels down to declare his love for her, and she gets up and leaves. Isabel walks quickly, as troubled as the wind in the trees, and takes refuge in a house. This, then, is our first encounter with this wild, headstrong and idealistic character.

Light years away from her previous performance, Suzanne Stone Maretto in *To Die For*, Kidman does not stare at the camera to recite her monologues with a smile, but looks serious and punctuates her replies with silences. She whispers and frequently looks away. The actress takes on an American accent once again and she is not afraid to emphasize her character's lack of finesse – she sniffs her boots after a day out walking, for example. When she rejects Caspar Goodwood (Viggo Mortensen), she pushes the door closed with her foot in an almost masculine way, without getting up from her chair, from disdain or laziness.

Although the film is based on a largely psychological novel, Kidman, it is interesting to note, pulls Isabel toward the trivial and worldly. More than simply a mind or a face, she has a real physicality: she gets up quickly, with a vivacity that is often found in Campion's actresses. By virtue of her furtive interpretation, Kidman is the perfect soloist for the part her director has given her. She portrays an exile – in every sense of the word – who leaves her surroundings sometimes as quickly as she entered

them, apparently wanting to escape from herself. Perhaps the attention from men is too oppressive, even if they are genuinely in love with her – as is Caspar, who confesses pleadingly, 'I hate to lose sight of you!' She claims not to want to be 'a mere sheep in the flock', like those single women waiting to be 'captured' (a word she uses at the beginning of the film). From the outset, Isabel wants to remain independent, outside the restrictions of convention and logic, a stance that pushes her, fatally, toward an irrational choice: loving a difficult man who treats her harshly.

After the departure of Caspar, who caresses her chin in silence before taking his leave, Isabel strokes her cheek and lets out a small sigh. Despite her obvious pride, tinged with a fake cold indifference, we understand that his young, wild, independent woman is actually not at all insensible to the desire of men, but that she intends to be the sole author of her own happiness, to make her own choices, without being forced into anything. With her head nestled against the floral wallpapered wall, her body sways, like a flower blown gently by the wind. Isabel touches her fingers to her skin and her lips and gradually enters a sort of trance, eyes open or closed, moving from side to side as though in a waltz. Before us, she steadily surrenders herself to pleasure, brushing her forehead and eyes against the fringes

on the canopy of her four-poster bed (as though she were confusing them with a man's hair), then looks ahead of her, with a fixed gaze. We imagine she has just seen someone out of frame. Isabel sits down on the bed, stretches out her arm, as Caspar had done a few minutes earlier, as by way of invitation. To the viewer's surprise, Caspar's hand takes hold of hers. Isabel lies back on the bed (which is also covered with flowers) and lets herself be kissed. To our amazement, we discover, in a lateral camera movement, Lord Warburton, who is embracing the young woman's knee. The camera then goes back to Isabel's face, next to which we now see Ralph Touchett, who is contemplating her. Kidman manages to help us understand that the appearance of these three men in the young woman's bedroom is a fantasy. And it is Isabel's fantasy itself, rather than the music, that brings the episode to an end. At the words 'I love you', spoken off-screen by one of the three lovers, Isabel stops moaning and writhing. She gets up and the three men vanish into thin air. Is it these words that have suddenly cooled her desire, or the impossibility of knowing which of the three men spoke them to her? With her successive visions, linked in the film by dreamlike sequences, Isabel seems to be announcing the future birth of cinema, and notably the experiments of the feminist filmmaker Germaine Dulac. Furthermore, by projecting her fantasies onto the world, she herself becomes a *camera obscura*.

A Graphic Composition

Campion and Kidman seem to have taken the title *The Portrait of a Lady* quite literally. Together, they work on textures, tones and lighting. In certain scenes the actress seems to be dancing with light beams (notably in the scene of the kiss with Osmond) and the camera movements that support the story. Only a shadow of herself, Isabel frequently appears in silhouette. The long focal length blurs the background, thereby accentuating her isolation; and the *chiaroscuro* which surrounds her emphasizes this in-between state. She appears backlit, which emphasizes the livid aspect of her hair.

Isabel's sidelong glances and bowed head are at one with the tilted frames favoured by the director, but are surprising within the context of a period drama. The character seems to be in search of new perspectives on the world. Even Kidman's body is often split within the frame, by means of optical effects, shadows and the play of mirrors. Her clothes, like a series of skins that she inhabits, seem to envelop her with different attitudes, depending on the place and circumstances of the story. When she begins to get involved with Osmond, she is wearing a blue dress and she waxes lyrical, speaking about this man as though he were Prince Charming. This is the first time in the film that she has expressed herself in this way. Her entourage think that she has let herself down,

Disturbed by Caspar Goodwood (Viggo Mortensen), who has touched her cheek, Isabel indulges in a fantasy, which takes the form of sensual caresses from the man she has just refused.

Opposite: Dangerously manipulative, Gilbert Osmond seduces the young woman during her trip to Italy.

Following pages: At the convent, where Isabel has come to visit Gilbert's daughter, Pansy (Valentina Cervi), Madame Merle (Barbara Hershey) attempts to open Isabel's eyes to her husband's nature.

**Opposite:** Before the marriage, when her cousin, Henrietta Stackpole (Mary-Louise Parker), spoke to her about her many suitors during a visit to the museum, Isabel contradicted her, expressing her desire for perfection and romanticism.

Jane Campion's long focal length accentuates the character's isolation. Her clothes seem to imbue her with different attitudes, depending on the place and circumstances of the story.

**Following pages:** Isabel seems to be in search of new perspectives on the world. Even her body is often split within the frame, by means of optical effects, shadows and the play of mirrors.

when in fact she has never appeared so radiant, in terms of colours and expressiveness.

## Mortification and Resurrection

At the beginning of *The Portrait of a Lady*, Isabel is like a vibrant plant in a humid environment. Here Kidman is capable of being moved to tears in a split second. Then we discover the dry ruins of Italy, with its dismembered statues. Isabel has lost a child (as had Campion before the beginning of the shoot). In a brief shot, she touches a small sculpted hand with her fingertips. Dressed in black, almost embalmed, like a doll, she is beginning to turn to stone. The parties she organizes are like funeral wakes. Her hair is braided, imprisoned. She now resembles an ice queen. Locked away, due to her own choice, in an unhappy marriage, she is losing her lustre. The female characters in this film are as much at fault as they are victims: as is the case with Madame Merle (Barbara Hershey), a hurt but manipulative woman.

Many powerful images reflect this general gradual decomposition, which is portrayed as being almost like a flagellation. On a tree-lined path, surrounded by mist, Isabel stands still, like a dead tree in the row, a long way from the flowering tree that she was at the beginning of the film. At another sombre moment, she wants to flee, but her husband, who is trying to control her

psychologically, is opposed to her leaving. Isabel at last realizes that she is trapped in this marriage that she so long desired and that Osmond seduced her to take advantage of her wealth. Blue like a corpse, she bangs her head against the walls and puts her hands to her temples. In a final attempt to save herself, she decides to leave, break free from her husband and return to England. It is the return of rain and steam. The young woman lets loose her hair, voices what is in her heart to those she loves and rediscovers her smile and the spring in her step. Tragically, the man she finally recognizes she has always loved, her cousin Ralph, is dying. She lies down beside him, never as alive as she is here, embracing a dying man (the inversion of the scene of her first kiss with Osmond). At the end of the film, we see her running again. However, instead of taking refuge in the house, she stops on the threshold and breathes a sigh of relief.

In the end, it is perhaps Campion who best sums up this female character and the complexity that the actress had to face: 'Initially, Isabel has such a high opinion of herself that she thinks she can manipulate others. In reality, because of her ambition, it is she who becomes manipulable, and thus manipulated… She believes she yearns for intellectual and spiritual life, that she should devote herself to a career, while in fact she dreams only of great passions. She doesn't really know herself and so can love only an illusion. *The Portrait of a Lady* is a young woman's

journey into hell, her encounter with darkness, and her awakening to consciousness. At the end, she may have found love, but most importantly, she has learned to know herself. This woman will never again cheat. In her own way, she is as opinionated as the other heroines I've filmed.'[51] In *The Second Sex* (a work well known to Kidman), Simone de Beauvoir wonders who can speak with any relevance about women: 'Man is at once judge and party to the case: but so is woman. What we need is an angel – neither man nor woman – but where shall we find one?'[52] Perhaps this is found at the cinema, where the director and her actress paint a portrait of a heroine at variance with her times, describing the Victorian woman as well as the determined woman, in an ambivalence that is disturbing and uncertain as well as creative.

Mixed Reactions

For David Thomson, '[...] once you have gone so far to inhabit a character like Isabel Archer, the harder it is – not just technically, but in your own spirit – to go back to anything trivial, cute and seductive again. An actress can alter the way in which we see her in one show. But she has to realize that that changes our future expectations, too. If you touch an author like Henry James, or a husband like Gilbert Osmond, you are changed for life, and pretending to be sunshine will convince no one.'[53] Before the release of

*The Portrait of a Lady*, the actress declared, 'This film means more to me than any film I've made. And I know it does to Jane, too. Some films you make which you can walk away from. This is one we're very protective of. We're out there feeling that we have to shield the baby. Protect the baby!'[54]

After the success of *The Piano*, *The Portrait of a Lady* universally disappointed both spectators and critics. As *Télérama* said of it, 'Hair cropped short, pale faced, and with jaws clenched since September, Jane Campion is on the defensive. At the last Venice Film Festival, *The Portrait of a Lady*, her fourth feature film, left most critics unsatisfied. It was a hard knock for the director, who has continued to accumulate awards and tributes.'[55]

Despite the challenging craftsmanship of the film, a role taken from a literary classic and her very nuanced performance, Kidman did not gain recognition either, except from a few rare critics. For Claude Baignères, 'Jane Campion has brought together for the lead roles actors who are totally at the top of their game. Both arrogant and mysterious, devious by dint of seeming too honest, John Malkovich portrays with infinite subtlety the rock on which Nicole Kidman will sharpen her enthusiastic good will. She is splendid, with no other protection than her desire for independence, her matchless beauty, her passion to make her own way in the world, taking

When Isabel finally breaks free from her husband, she returns to England. Tragically, the man she finally recognizes she has always loved, her cousin Ralph (Martin Donovan), is dying. She lies down beside him, never as alive as she is here, embracing a dying man.

Opposite: Campion and Kidman, whom the director met as a teenager.

Kidman has forged strong emotional bonds with filmmakers such as George Miller, Stanley Kubrick, Baz Luhrmann and Lars von Trier, but her friendship with Jane Campion remains the closest, despite the fact that only one film currently bears witness to it (a second, *In the Cut*, was produced and supported by the actress in 2003).

Kidman met the director when she was a teenager in Australia. She recalls their first meeting with amusement: 'She wanted me for her first short film when she was at film school. I was supposed to kiss another girl! I was fourteen and I refused. I was in a [theatre] school and I imagined myself with long hair performing in *Gone with the Wind*. Today I would have accepted!'[b]

Ten years later, their reunion took place in dramatic circumstances: 'When she offered me the role of Isabel Archer [in *The Portrait of a Lady*], she had just lost her first child, Jasper, shortly after his birth, and she had to delay filming.'[c] The actress describes their personal and artistic understanding with great affection: 'I love her; we're very close; we see each other a lot. She is very psychological, hypersensitive and emotional. Jane gets inside your head and under your skin. I don't know how she does it, but it's a gift. She will ask you a question, watch you, then play games. I remember going walking in Italy for four days with her. We used to hitchhike, buy bread and cheese, stop in strange places and climb trees. That's Jane for you. When I am working with her, she makes use of her knowledge of me and of our friendship.'[d]

Meanwhile, Jane has said that Nicole is 'a very intelligent woman, who doesn't like to advertise it, even displays a lot of reserve… She also has a great capacity to express various emotions very quickly. She's really one of the princesses of our generation.'[e]

everything on herself, especially her mistakes. And sometimes those of others.'[56] But there were neither awards nor nominations, and little praise from critics worldwide, who clearly preferred Barbara Hershey's perverse performance in the role of Madame Merle. In the United States, in particular, some of the criticism was harsh: 'Kidman, so good in *To Die For*, is wan and uninteresting here... Kidman's uncanny resemblance to Elizabeth Montgomery in *Bewitched* makes taking her seriously a real chore.'[57]

Yet, over the years, Kidman's Isabel has taken root, notably with Agnès Peck, who paints a sensitive portrait of the actress in *Positif*: 'The actress's physical traits became an expressive issue... Kidman's height and thinness, highlighted by her stretched-out silhouette, and the length of her exaggeratedly dangling arms, suggest a touching fragility, an awkwardness even, in the same way that the gentle tapering of her long white hands, with their caressing inflections, intensify the heroine's lassitude and poignant grace. Her whole face is a picture of passionate intensity, reflected in contrasts, the paleness of her complexion enhanced by the frizzy mass of her auburn hair (a sign of a passionate, rather wild nature), a mixture of seductive innocence and languid eroticism (the wispy halo, the sinuosities that are evocative of the vague grace of Pre-Raphaelite models).'[58]

Whatever the feedback from critics, Kidman, who in Australia during the 1970s used to accompany her mother to feminist meetings, was proud to have participated in this film, a significant work about women: 'I used to watch these women lying on the carpet, talking. Their discussions had a huge impact on me.'[59] In *The Portrait of a Lady* she was also surrounded by experienced female stars, who included Shelley Winters as Mrs Touchett and Shelley Duvall as Countess Gemini, two faces that had been enhanced in the past by a certain Stanley Kubrick (Winters in *Lolita*, 1962, and Duvall in *The Shining*, 1980). It was like a passing of the torch, for it was with this same demiurge that Kidman was about to embark on another extraordinary artistic adventure concerning another portrait of a woman, this time a contemporary one.

Opposite: Isabel is a prisoner of appearances. '*The Portrait of a Lady* is a young woman's journey into hell, her encounter with darkness and awakening to consciousness', Campion explains.

61

# 4

# Alice Harford

*Eyes Wide Shut* (1999)
Stanley Kubrick

'I think it changed the way I view films. It gave me a belief in the purity of filmmaking, in the art form of making a film. And that however long it takes, whatever you have to go through, you're making a film. It's about getting lost in that world and it's exquisite when it happens.'[60]
Nicole Kidman, 2000

Throughout the 1990s, Nicole Kidman and Tom Cruise (who were amassing critical and commercial hits) formed one of the most glamorous couples in the history of cinema. Their dominance of the movie scene drew the attention of Stanley Kubrick, who watched all their films (particularly Kidman's) for months before contacting them. He wished to adapt Arthur Schnitzler's novella *Traumnovelle* (*Dream Story*), published in 1926, which discloses the fantasies of a married couple. Middle-class New Yorkers Alice Harford (Nicole Kidman) and Dr Bill Harford (Tom Cruise) see their relationship turned upside down when Alice reveals to her husband the erotic feelings she once had for another man, a desire so strong that she could have left everything for him. This revelation unnerves Bill, who naively thought that only men felt these sorts of desires. Until this point he had been leading a fairly routine existence, both professionally and personally (as a renowned doctor, faithful husband and loving father), but now he begins to gradually tip over into a double life: he flirts with a prostitute then dons a disguise to participate in an orgy. The film follows the wanderings of this couple who are entangled in a web of erotic games, pretences and doubts about the foundations of their relationship.

## Kidman and Kubrick

Kidman, who was afraid of not being equal to working with the legendary director, met Kubrick first at his home, a manor house in St Albans, north of London, where she did a reading of the film's two great monologues. She remembers their first interview: 'He has the most extraordinary eyes you've ever seen on a human. They look at you, and they have this quite mischievous quality. They have a great sense of having lived. I was just terrified that he would

fire me. I thought he'd take one look at me and say, "Gosh, what was I thinking? This woman is not right for the role." I was very nervous around him. Partly because I was so in awe of him and then just because I have in the film two very big monologues that I thought were gonna be very difficult. There's my insecurities as an actor.'[61]
A few weeks later, Kubrick finally gave the project the green light. Kidman was ecstatic. Admittedly, the eighteen weeks originally planned for the shoot turned into fifteen months, but this unusually long collaboration enabled the actress to forge close ties with her character and with the director. 'Over the course of time, I became so confident with him. He gave me such confidence as an actor and really allowed me such freedom as an actor. He'd say, "You've done a few takes. Now just do what you wanna do." I'd heard stories about him being incredibly controlling. At certain times, he was controlling. At other times, he allowed me to really just get lost in Alice. Over the course of the year and a half, I became that woman.'[62]

Kidman chose the colour of the curtains in the Harford's bedroom, the books on the bedside table and installed her own personal belongings (make-up, clothes, etc.). Kubrick, amazed by her dedication, declared 'that he had never worked, before Nicole Kidman, with an actress who wanted additional takes'.[63] In return, Kidman underlined the way Kubrick allowed her to develop her performance: 'Stanley was always waiting for something to happen. He wasn't as interested in "naturalistic" acting as he was in something that, for whatever reason, surprised him or piqued his interest. That's when he'd go, "Now we're onto something." He was always interested in exploring all facets of things. It was the most wonderful experience because you didn't ever walk away from the set feeling "Oh, I didn't get it. If only he'd let me have one more, we would've discovered something." He made sure he discovered all there was to discover in the material.'[64] Won over and transformed, she added, 'I was very relaxed. So a lot of the time when the cameras were on, I wasn't even aware. Partly, you're tired, which is actually a good thing when you're acting because it means that you're not trying to produce emotions or thinking this is how it should be;

it just happens. It just sort of comes out of you. It's very hard to explain. It's something only a few people who have worked with Stanley understand.'[65]

Behind the Statue, a Whirl of Emotions

The first sequence of *Eyes Wide Shut* is one of the most symbolic in the film. Kidman, completely naked, seems to be undulating, like an ancient Greek statue in movement, to the rhythm of Shostakovich's 'Waltz 2' from his *Second Jazz Suite* (1938). She gently removes the straps of her dress, allowing it to casually glide down her body to the floor and letting us catch a glimpse of her bottom. She then steps free of it, as though she were dancing a waltz in front of a mirror: she is both a vision and in the vision.

Pam Cook notes that 'The brief glimpse of Kidman naked recalls her 1998 appearance in *The Blue Room*, David Hare's adaptation of Schnitzler's play *Der Reigen*, filmed by Max Ophuls as *La Ronde* (1950), in which she and Iain Glen played different characters involved in a series of sexual encounters. In one scene, Kidman appeared naked in back view for a few moments as Glen slowly dressed her – this caused a sensation and contributed to the play's critical and box-office success.'[66]

A few moments later, glasses perched on her nose, Alice is sitting on the toilet but wearing a different dress. We assume that she has changed several times before choosing this particular evening dress. She seems to have felt around, reflected, looked and compared. Bill, on the other hand, does not know where he has put his wallet. Unlike him, she is in a state of reflection and projection right from the beginning. He sees nothing, answering her without even looking at her. She stands up and wipes her bottom, in full view of the audience. Is the film's main character the one played by superstar Tom Cruise? We begin to doubt it.

In the following scene, at the ball, Alice walks in a detached, elegant way. She seems to float, gracefully, but her attitude reflects a hint of boredom. She is clearly enthralled by neither the splendour nor the guests of the party she has been invited to. She nonchalantly takes a glass of champagne, then goes to the bathroom: Alice is constantly either urinating or drinking at the beginning of the film. A mature guest then sets about seducing her. He deliberately drinks from the young woman's glass, as though to taste her, then takes hold of her arm in a determined way in order to kiss her hand and lead her onto the dance floor. Often seen from behind or filmed from a distance, Alice seems to be viewed as no more than an object, a figurine rather than a human being, who has not yet shown her true face. We learn simply that she used to manage an art gallery in SoHo. Her job is to expose, to see.

Kidman has undertaken nude scenes in several of her films; early works, such as *Windrider* (Vincent Monton, 1986) and *Dead Calm* (Phillip Noyce, 1989), included partial nudity and *Billy Bathgate* (Robert Benton, 1991) required a full-frontal performance. She is equally comfortable with the sensitive practice of recreating sex on screen, as demonstrated in *To Die For* (Gus Van Sant, 1995) as well as *Eyes Wide Shut* (Stanley Kubrick, 1999). In *Birthday Girl* (Jez Butterworth, 2001), she is naked and tied to the bed during a sex scene with Ben Chaplin's character. She also makes love with Clive Owen during bombing raid, her body covered in dust, in *Hemingway & Gellhorn* (Philip Kaufman, 2012). She recalled: 'When Philip Kaufman explained to me that there would be a number of sex scenes, I asked lots of questions in order to assure myself that they fitted with the turbulent relationship between the two characters. Hemingway and Gellhorn didn't just exchange ideas; they made love, often and everywhere, including right in the middle of a bombing raid. And then I trusted him, and when I establish that sort of relationship of trust with a director, I surrender myself.'[f] The same year, Kidman pushed the boundaries of sexuality on screen even further in the controversial *The Paperboy* (Lee Daniels, 2012). To everyone's amazement (on the very first day of the shoot, Kidman and John Cusack's character engaged in a violent sex scene), the dishevelled actress openly masturbates and later, in another scene, urinates on Zac Efron. 'Before making this film, I had said to friends that I really wanted to make something raw, savage: no one thinks of me for that sort of role', she explained. 'Well, I certainly wasn't disappointed! Everything is sanitized nowadays. People judge you very easily, very quickly.'[g]

In a path that is more daring and unsettling than the roles taken by Sharon Stone for example (compare the rape scenes of *Dogville* with the banal eroticism of *Basic Instinct*), Kidman has, in her own way, rewritten female sexuality on screen. In the words of Samuel Blumenfeld, 'no other Hollywood star of this stature, with such a long, such a rich career, has been required to undertake nude scenes so often on screen, to quietly live out her sexuality in front of the camera, to expose her libido so naturally to the audience.'[h]

Opposite: In *The Paperboy* (2012) by Lee Daniels, Kidman pushes the boundaries of sexuality on screen even further, playing the role of a woman who openly masturbates, and urinates on one of her sexual partners.

Above: That night, when the couple arrive home, the whirl of emotions continues in front of a mirror, but the pair soon resume their usual routine. Alice becomes the woman as object, in all the banality of her day-to-day life.

Following pages: Stanley Kubrick directing Nicole Kidman and Madison Eginton, who plays Helena, the Harfords' daughter.

And, indeed, she spots her husband talking with two beautiful young women. She smiles, almost excited, but is not in the least offended. Her husband, on the other hand, has not yet seen that she is dancing with someone else. With her eyes raised, Kidman has a look that is very Kubrickian, almost perverse. Obviously drunk, she throws her head back and simpers during this flirtation with a stranger, but in a disinterested way, not taking the party seriously. Basically, she is playing the seduction game. The orchestra for the evening finishes the piece they have been playing and Alice awakes from her reverie. She opens her eyes, detaches herself from her partner and, with a rather sad smile, shows him her wedding ring to break the spell: she is a prisoner in her marriage. She kisses her index finger and places it on the stranger's lips, falsely flirtatious. She plays with her fingers, dominating her admirer and the situation. She is neither a doll that can be manipulated at will nor an easy woman.

Back in the marital home, the whirl of emotions continues in front of a mirror (that of *Alice in Wonderland*?), with the now-famous images of the couple naked. Alice is seen from behind. She removes her earrings and, with graceful gestures, opens herself up completely to abandon herself to Kubrick's camera. Bill joins her and kisses her while she leads the dance. However, the following day the couple resume their usual routine: the husband leaves to go to work while

the wife takes care of their daughter, whom the mother teaches, by encouraging her to imitate her, how to wrap a present for her father. Again, Alice becomes the woman as object, in all the banality of her day-to-day life: she puts on deodorant and sniffs her armpits – a small detail that recurs in Kidman's other films. Kidman knows how to neutralize her elegance in order to establish her characters as ordinary women rather than goddesses. Alice yawns while Bill watches football. Then she returns to the bathroom mirror, which seems to be calling to her. We sense that she needs to talk, to express herself, to reflect (on herself). She is full of doubts. Everything seems to be going round in circles, in a whirl, an endless waltz. She takes her head in her hands, an idea in her head. We are suddenly right beside her, almost inside her head. She takes a packet of cannabis out of the medicine cabinet then looks up.

## Mind Games

Lying languidly on the bed, Alice smokes a joint, her eyes closed. Gradually she opens them, as though she were waking up. Her ideas take shape. She speaks slowly, detaching her words, her diction in keeping with her movements. For the first time in the film, she uses the crude word 'fuck', as though opening the door, or taking the lid off Pandora's box, of the discussion and adventures to come. She questions her husband

about his fantasies, but his replies do not satisfy her. She strokes her lips with her finger. She screws up her eyes, indicating suspicion. Alice is not fooled. Stretched out on the bed like a doll, the prisoner of her husband who looks down on her, she quickly rids herself of his hold of her. We see her then in a transparent top and panties. She unfurls herself and walks backward, while the camera is drawn to Kidman like a moth to a flame. She straightens up, staggers and leans against the wall. He remains seated. She has her hand on her hip and starts to take control of the conversation. Almost masculine, without a bra and with muscled thighs, Alice amuses herself by pinching her nipples, alluding to her husband's patients. Then, when Bill declares that men and women approach sex differently, she stands up and points her finger at him as though it were a revolver. Yes, yes, the result of 'millions of years of evolution'. 'If you men only knew!' Faced with her husband's somewhat ridiculous self-confidence, Alice finally bursts out laughing. Her body, literally doubled up, is much more expressive than that of her husband, motionless, stunned, transformed into an object of derision.

But the final blow is yet to come: Alice, until this point fairly ethereal, sits down on the floor, quite dismayed but gradually pulling herself together. She clears her throat, while watching her husband in order to gauge the situation,

and positions herself with her back against the wall, her hair dishevelled. She then tells him about how she fantasized about a stranger the previous summer and launches into a sensual half-murmured monologue. Alice hypnotizes her husband, casting a spell on him that turns him to stone. She separates her words to give them emphasis, and announces to Bill that she was 'ready to give up everything' for this handsome stranger. She pronounces the sentence through clenched teeth in a way that is almost monstrous, carnivorous. Alice is enjoying this confession, which is so traumatizing for her husband.

As Cook comments, 'Throughout the film, Alice is depicted as a figure, even a figment in the film's dream narrative, which is presented from Bill's point of view. It gets complicated when Alice's dream enters the story. Suddenly she's the subject of her own fantasy (if it is hers) at the same time as being a character/object in Bill's. This is the key to Bill's identity crisis: in his psyche a battle for dominance is played out in which gender roles are confirmed, tested and overturned.'[67]

The actress enunciates her words slowly, as though this fantasy has been consuming her for a long time, as though Alice was talking in her sleep or under hypnosis. The scene ends with a phone ringing, which breaks the spell and makes the young woman sigh, her face wearing a weary smile. The routine of daily life

Opposite: Toward the end of the film, Bill returns home in the early hours. He watches his wife laughing in her sleep then listens as she tells him about the nightmare she has just had. Kidman delivers this second monologue in a bluish light, and finishes up breaking down in tears.

Above: In the final scene, which takes place in a toy store, Alice gets back on her feet and leads the way for this couple, who have clearly been marked by these ordeals.

is resumed, but she has introduced doubt into the marriage, and her husband, until then blind, will not stop brooding over it. In this very long scene, a masterpiece in itself, Kidman, alone, has created a psychological tension nuanced by pauses, dislocations and bewitching glances. As she sums it up, 'it was the first time that my sensuality was at the centre of a film, not a peripheral element, but the subject of the film, and it was Kubrick's idea'.[68]

## The Total Woman

Bill returns home in the early hours, after a series of various adventures, including a dalliance with adultery and voyeurism. He goes into the bedroom and watches his wife laughing in her sleep. When he wakes her up the viewers are not quite sure whether Alice has invented the nightmare she relates to him, in which they were both naked to the world (a reference to the original short story, which deals with shame and social nudity). This monologue, Alice's second, portrays not a fantasy but the character's subconscious. Kidman plays the scene in a bluish light, reminiscent of the chilly atmosphere of a morgue, rather than in a more orange-tinged glow *à la* Douglas Sirk. She is more serious, colder, something has changed. This time, it is she who is careworn. She finishes up breaking down in tears.

Later, Bill's secret mask (part of the disguise he used earlier) lies on his pillow, next to Alice's sleeping face. She perhaps symbolically embodies fantasy, two-timing and infidelity. Finding the mask there, Bill, in turn, begins to cry. His tears wake Alice, like an echo or a symbolic mirror. The following morning, her hair dishevelled, the young woman is defeated, distraught at having learned of her husband's escapades. But, in the final scene, which takes place in a toy store, she gets back on her feet and leads the way for this couple, who have clearly been marked by these adult ordeals. In a shot reverse shot, her daughter shows her a Barbie doll (with which both the character of Alice and Kidman herself have been compared). Not really amused, she sighs. Her glasses on, she is seeing clearly again, while Bill moves forward cautiously, like a child. Once more it is Kidman who brings all the emotion to this scene, as well as the line, 'Maybe I think we should be grateful. Grateful that we've managed to survive through all of our adventures. Whether they were real, or only a dream … The important thing is we're awake now …' Alice is the gravitational centre of the film. We understand that she has carried Bill on her shoulders, both physically (she is present in the first and the last shots) and through her reflections. It is she who utters the last line in the film: 'Fuck!' Essentially, Kidman can perhaps be seen as the ultimate total woman, who, as Edgar Morin said in relation to

Ava Gardner, 'lives totally in accordance with the soul and sex'.[69]

## Media Impact

The extreme complexity of Kidman's performance was remarked on by filmmaker Pascale Ferran, who directed the voice actors of the French version: 'The most difficult part to dub was that of Nicole Kidman, who has long monologues that undergo considerable psychological evolutions in the course of a single scene, fits of laughter, crying spells, a scansion that changes constantly …'[70] For the trickier passages, Kidman cried for several hours before the take in order to achieve the powerful close-ups of her psychological collapse, particularly after Bill's revelation. 'I look at my face and I go, "Oh my gosh, I look so ravaged." But I love that I look ravaged!,'[71] she comments.

Rumours surrounding the shooting of *Eyes Wide Shut* (numerous gruelling takes, non-simulated sex scenes), which threatened the reputation of the decade's star couple, sent the press into a flurry for several months. Furthermore, Kubrick's sudden death, a few weeks before the film's release, added to the media hubbub. On 5 July 1999, Kidman and Cruise even made the headlines of *Time Magazine*, a rare honour for a Hollywood couple. The immediate reception from critics, which was probably undermined by the high level of anticipation the film had generated, was mixed. For the *Chicago Tribune*, it was 'a masterpiece',[72] while *The Independent* described it as a failure, in which 'Kidman's role in *Eyes Wide Shut* is to talk dirty from beginning to end… which shows Kidman – not Cruise, of course – get up off the toilet and wipe her bottom… *Eyes Wide Shut* inhabits an infantile fantasy world in which female desire, once let off its leash, is exhibitionist, masochistic and indiscriminately promiscuous.'[73] *Télérama* questioned the way in which Kubrick viewed women: 'One is tempted to reply, with the exception of a passing nymphette: like statues. Statues in high heels in the fuck room, recumbent statues in the mortuary, a (barely) more mobile statue in a camisole with Nicole Kidman. As though the director, at the same moment that he is enthralled by bodies, turns them to stone. It is in this subtle interplay between the gaze of a salacious child and that of an aesthete uncle that the novelty and perhaps the value of this film lies …'[74] For *Libération*, 'one gets bored in this laboratory. Cruise and Kidman, probably exhausted or losing their bearings with the number of takes, often seem dazed like rats in their cage …'[75] However, time seems to have ruled in favour of the film's beauty and relevance, as was noted, for example, by *Positif,* who called the actress 'the authentic Kubrickian *hero* of the film… In a charming role reversal, it is in effect the woman who, in this last work, reveals with an ambivalent seduction the ironic aggression, the desire for power and the destructive pleasure that have hitherto been the prerogative of masculine heroes.'[76]

In any event, for Kidman, on a personal level, there was a before and an after *Eyes Wide Shut*. Samuel Blumenfeld says that, after the shoot, 'Schnitzler became Nicole Kidman's *idée fixe*. [In] *The Blue Room*, [she] briefly revealed her bottom, causing a sensation that went far beyond her work as an actress.' Ironically, Kubrick's last public appearance, just before his heart attack, was, according to Kidman, at a performance of *The Blue Room*.[77] For Christiane Kubrick, the director's widow, the experience of the film remains a memorable one: 'Nicole and Tom spent lots of time here during the shoot. We remained very close. The film had an impact on their relationship because to enact those roles they had to analyse and dissect them. And because Stanley could have been their grandfather, they confided in him. A strong relationship of trust grew up between them. Stanley believed in them both and they, trusting him, gave him everything they had to give. Stanley told me he was touched because he felt that, not content simply to take off their clothes, they tore off their skin, baring their souls completely.'[78] The result was that, over the months, Kidman and Cruise's marriage began to reveal cracks. Kidman, however, continued to work on a series of films and in late 1999 returned to Australia to shoot a flamboyant love story, in which she dances and sings: *Moulin Rouge!*

Alice Harford, the gravitational centre of the film. Not only is she is present in the first and the last scenes, but she also dominates throughout with her quick wit.

# 5

# Satine

*Moulin Rouge!* (2001)
Baz Luhrmann

'I knew that this film was going to change my life and my career because you don't often get the chance to sing, dance and act at the same time.'[79] Nicole Kidman, 2001

A new century was beginning and, with it, a new set of circumstances for Kidman, both personally (her marriage was coming to an end) and professionally. Lots of roles were being offered to her, outside Hollywood, including that in *Moulin Rouge!* 'Everything was happening at the same time, both good and bad,' she recalls. 'I was playing at the theatre in New York, and Baz [Luhrmann] sent me two dozen red roses with a note saying, "I have a marvellous role for you: she sings, she dances, she loves, she dies. Call me." But he didn't give me the role just like that. I had to audition for six hours and I waited a week for his answer. He made me jump, dance, sing; I was ridiculous. Next he brought me a book, full of photos and documents. No screenplay. Then he talked to me about the story through his own visual world. Baz is someone whose passion is contagious. I did the film for him.'[80]

Kidman plays Satine, a popular dancer and courtesan at the heart of belle-époque Montmartre. She falls in love with a writer, Christian (Ewan McGregor), while she is supposed to be the exclusive mistress of an investor, the Duke (Richard Roxburgh), who could enable her to leave the cabaret and make her a famous actress. She therefore has to keep on her toes, juggling her artistic ambitions, her forbidden love and her failing health (which she keeps a secret). Suffice to say that this multifaceted character is tailor-made for Kidman, who excels in the art of double bluffing. Indeed, Satine could be seen as her most iconic role.

## An Exceedingly Physical Shoot

The actress had not worked in Australia since making the little-known *Flirting* (John Duigan, 1991), ten years earlier. This return to familiar ground extricated her for a time from her personal worries in the United States. The cast shut themselves away in Sydney for a few weeks to discuss, rehearse and sing, much like in the rehearsals portrayed in the film. Its musical director, Marius de Vries, recalls: 'The atmosphere was chaotic and exciting. Exhausting. Not much sleep. A lot of red wine. A bit of absinthe (to help us learn about the period, of course). And frequent anxiety attacks faced with the enormity of the task.'[81] But everyone was ready and highly motivated when filming began. Faced with John O'Connell's choreography and Luhrmann and cinematographer Donald McAlpine's cameras, the actress let her hair down, literally. On set, the director was the first to be blown away by her commitment: 'Working with Nicole, I met someone warm, crazy and funny. I mean, she's a hundred feet tall, incredibly beautiful and also very alive and capable of doing mad things. I believe that she's going to surprise a lot of people in a register that we didn't expect of her.'[82]

Each day this role of courtesan required three hours of preparation, including make-up, hair and costumes. The tight corsets were a trial for Kidman, restricting her dance movements, preventing her from moving as she wanted and leaving her body bruised. In addition to mastering the dance routines, the actress chose to sing while acting, even though a soundtrack had been pre-recorded in the studio. Admittedly, she had done ballet as a little girl, and appreciates music. However, although she likes to immerse herself in music that is in keeping with the roles she is playing, it was something else entirely to have to become a real performer before hundreds of people (including the film's cast, crew and extras): 'When I'm acting, I listen to music – jazz, rock or classical, whatever is good for my character. For me, singing in front of an audience is much more difficult than acting. I admit that it was a real challenge to work under Baz Luhrmann's direction.'[83]

Confronting, as she often does, what she was afraid of, the star tackled the task head on and refused a double, notably in the scene, at the beginning of the film, where she is suspended on a trapeze. During a rehearsal, she fell and hurt herself, and filming had to be postponed for a fortnight. Kidman returned to shoot the film with weakened ankles and knees but, as her frail character is told, 'the show must go on' (a reference to Queen's song about Freddie Mercury, which forms part of the film's soundtrack).

The role of Satine, a popular dancer and courtesan at the heart of belle-époque Montmartre, was tailor-made for Kidman, who excels in the art of double bluffing.

Putting her pain to one side, the actress fervently picked up her role again, unable to stop working. Caught up in the part, she later admitted, 'The characters that I have played continue to resonate in me. That's why I didn't want *Moulin Rouge!* to end. I had never acted in a great love story, so pure and so simple. Being able to be in love every day made me radiant.'[84]

To Be or Not to Be an Actress

Kidman's first appearance, a quarter of an hour into the film, is spectral. An angel floating in the air, an acrobat on her trapeze, she dominates Catherine Martin's sets, which are anchored in a fantasized version of turn-of-the-century Paris inspired by *The Blue Angel* (Josef von Sternberg, 1930), *Gilda* (Charles Vidor, 1946) and *Cabaret* (Bob Fosse, 1972). With costumes designed by Martin, Satine wears a Marlene Dietrich-style top hat adorned with a diamond-encrusted hatband. At first half-lit, she is revealed to us in a succession of close-ups of her face, displaying effects worthy of Marilyn Monroe, making best use of her long, black-glove-clad arms. Satine looks downs on her spectators from her great height. All light and sparkle, she circles above a scene that encompasses the whole space, where the audience stands in silence, in contrast to the first minutes of the film. As soon as she makes her entrance, the crowd packed into the Moulin Rouge lift their eyes heavenward in unison, the light turns blue (an almost funereal hue). Satine appears, her eyes lowered, then looks straight at the camera, at us. This Kidman hallmark reveals a lot about the ambivalence that she likes to disseminate, as though, with it, the conventional barrier of the screen or stage were abolished, constantly reflecting on her status as an actress, something between fantasy and reality. We gaze into her eyes as intently as she looks into ours. She de-masks us in the darkened room and transforms us into dumbfounded objects.

A few moments later, she looks straight at the camera again, causing us to pause in the midst of the frenzied dance, and Satine tells herself and the viewers that she is going to be 'a real actress'. She pronounces the last word as if it is a dream tinged with sadness. It is, in any event, in this fleeting confidence that the self-reflective role about the acting profession is proclaimed. As Agnès Peck expounds: 'the film plays on the pleasure of collusion and recognition. Nicole Kidman "plays" the echoes of stars of a bygone era, skimming through the film lover's imaginary world, blending the sensual provocation of Rita Hayworth (in *Gilda*), the expressive eloquence of Greta Garbo's face (in her melodramatic roles) and Monroe's mix of innocence and eroticism…. The harsh make-up and lighting amplify the sensuality of the shot: the focus on the voluptuous red lips, the pale glaze of her skin and the troubled or dazzling clarity of her gaze.'[85]

As she sings 'Diamonds Are a Girl's Best Friend', the song that immortalized Monroe in *Gentlemen Prefer Blondes* (Howard Hawks, 1953), Satine wonders how best to seduce the Duke. What role should she play to achieve her ends? 'What's his type? Wilting flower? Bright and bubbly? Or smouldering temptress?' Satine can, in fact, put on any face, play any role, as is hinted at in the many mirror effects that continually split her body. She willingly plays, and indeed overplays, glamorous actresses and pin-up stars, provocatively and exuberantly raising an eyebrow. She crawls and writhes in pleasure on the animal skins on the floor. She wallows to the point of becoming a mere caricature of herself, provoking an amused smile in her audience. Kidman's comic ability, revealed in *To Die For*, is displayed here without restraint, and as rarely matched later, even in the few comedies that she made in the 2000s (such as Frank Oz's *The Stepford Wives*, 2004, and Nora Ephron's *Bewitched*, 2005). Her role in *Moulin Rouge!* marked a milestone in her career and gave her the opportunity to make an uninhibited foray into burlesque, albeit for only a few vignettes. This quirky fantasy suits her perfectly, particularly as there is a hint of danger about it: Satine plays the clown to seduce Christian, whom she believes is the Duke (endangering her original plan without realizing it), then saves appearances by improvising a play for the wealthy patron, gesticulating wildly.

As is often the case in Kidman's films, we see her in dangerous situations that she has to get out of. This humour/danger duality is a recurring theme, particularly in *Moulin Rouge!*, which is nevertheless a musical that is more ominous and darker than it at first appears. Satine's antics and bright smile betray an anxiety, an oppressive threat and a darker psychological context that make her less of a comic and more of a tragic figure. She would like to believe in love, succeed as a real actress and be in good health. But creating an appearance is the role assigned to her. When she simulates sex and plays up prostitution, which becomes confused with acting, she states loudly and clearly to Christian, 'I am a courtesan. I'm paid to make men believe what they want to believe.' Between lies and acts, Satine lets slip some truths, and Kidman has to manage a lot of breaks in the rhythm and tone, moving from burlesque to tragic love story, sometimes in just a few seconds (or so the editing would have us believe). This is notably the case when Harold Zidler (Jim Broadbent) surprises Satine and Christian, and they have to allay the Duke's suspicions. The role of Satine reflects the turmoil of a particular Parisian era and its follies, but also the madness of the world of entertainment.

**Kidman and Commercials**

For better or worse, the history of actors, both minor and major, goes hand in hand with the history of advertising. The young Australian began appearing in commercials in the 1980s (notably for an insurance company where her character was lying in a hospital bed in plaster). From the early 2000s, however, she began to forge significant relationships with the advertising industry. She made a Spanish commercial, directed by Alejandro Amenábar, for a chain of Spanish department stores, then an ad campaign for a video game. She has also touted Schweppes drinks, pronouncing the phrase, 'What did you expect?' (since taken up by Uma Thurman and Penélope Cruz). The commercial was considered distasteful by some because Kidman gulps her drink loudly in close-up. Over and above the financial rewards, these adverts are about the pleasure the actress takes in thwarting her own image, which is a habit integral to the way she manages her career and her personality – at once very direct, yet without appearing to be so.

In 2004, she agreed to represent the luxury watch brand Omega and, in the same year, made a very ambitious commercial, directed by Baz Luhrmann, for Chanel No. 5. With a budget of more than $40 million, this three-minute commercial not only provided a substantial fee for the actress (a quarter of the total budget), but also the chance to work with the team of *Moulin Rouge!* again. In this mini-film, accompanied by 'Clair de lune' by Claude Debussy, she plays a star who flees the limelight. Bordering on self-portrait, this radiant character has a troubling, ambiguous relationship with wealth and fame, oscillating between imprisonment and freedom, attraction and repulsion, confession and compromise.

Until very recently, Kidman continued to make commercials in different countries, notably for an Italian television channel, a Brazilian shopping mall, an Australian brand of vitamins and, recently, for an airline. Often made in almond-blossom pink hues, these parallel visions to her official filmography immortalize the actress's cosmetic beauty, feline gestures and bewitching gaze as much as her self-mockery. For some, however, they undermine her image and taint her artistic ambitions. According to these critics, Kidman has herself become a brand, a prefabricated, Photoshopped commodity. A commodity, however, that resolutely creates and narrates her own character – a mischievous courtesan seeking to stand out and survive at the very heart of the industry.

## Eurydice in the Show World

As the film progresses, Satine becomes embroiled in a complex game. She will soon have to pretend that she does not love Christian in order to protect him from the Duke's fury. But, for the first time, she is undone: she can no longer play-act and gives way to tears as the mask falls. Ironically, she chastises herself for having believed in something true (love), while her suitors were believing in her lies. Likened to a caged bird, as at the beginning of the film where she resembles a parakeet imprisoned in a feathered costume, Satine is composed of blue light, a shot that is reminiscent of that of Alice's haggard face at the end of *Eyes Wide Shut*. Kidman develops what she had learned and experienced in her previous film, seemingly making a sort of hallmark of her beautiful pale face ravaged by sorrow. But Satine has no choice. She must save Christian by lying about her feelings for him. She closes her eyes in concentration, as before going on stage, gathering her strength. When she opens them again, she is like a robot-woman ready to instantly obey the task she has been set or a little soldier prepared for self-sacrifice. Does this episode represent a mourning for pretending she does not love him, or a veiling of her sadness so that she gives nothing away?

The final sequence begins with a symbolic Hindu song, 'I Only Speak the Truth!'. Satine initiates an immense danse macabre. She tries to follow the choreography while sick both with love and physically. As she vibrates her body and her vocal chords, Kidman's performance is electrifying (perhaps in parallel with the electricity that surrounds her on stage, emphasizing its innovatory use in modern cities of the time). Peck observes: 'she has a way of immobilizing movement, of conjuring up moments of grace, prolonging the languid charm of a posture by means of the exquisite flexibility of an arm or hand. At the same time, this harmonious fluidity of line and movement is shot through with micro-tremors, which bring to mind delicate metaphors such as that of a butterfly trying to extricate itself from a sticky syrup.'[86]

Idolized as a goddess, Satine has become the property of her suitors, who hope, like the Duke, that she belongs to them – until they understand that they have been duped. Then we come to the film's final twist: while Christian is reproaching Satine for having made him believe she loved him, she finally decides to sing, on stage, in front of everyone, in order to tell him what she really feels. And it is through this public declaration that she reveals her innermost feelings. The performance becomes the truth. This is undoubtedly one of the metaphorical and emotional peaks of Kidman's work. And yet, this avowal that serves as the finale of *Moulin Rouge!* does not save the life of the courtesan. Like Orpheus, Christian is unable

Opposite and above:
The role of Satine gave
the actress the opportunity
to make an uninhibited foray
into burlesque, such as when
she plays the clown to seduce
Christian, whom she believes
is the Duke, then saves
appearances by improvising
a play for the wealthy patron,
gesticulating wildly.

Following pages: Kidman
in the final sequence,
a *dance macabre*, during
which Satine tries to follow
the choreography while being
physically ill and sick with love.

to deliver Satine, his Eurydice, from death. From her first to her last appearance she belongs to the shadowland: in shadow she appeared and in shadow she will perish.

## A Kaleidoscope of Reviews

*Moulin Rouge!*, presented as the opening film at the 2001 Cannes Film Festival, gave Kidman the chance to review her acting career: 'I feel safe when I am acting. Because I have a director in front of me to whom I can say, "This is what I feel, this is what I can give, help me." That's not the case in life: there is no one to hold your hand, you're on your own. It's reassuring to be on set, surrounded by a film crew. The problem is that I probably throw myself too deeply into my roles. I always end up ill, exhausted or injured. I don't know how to protect myself, either emotionally or physically.'[87] The actress took the opportunity to set the record straight with Hollywood, which she had been shunning for several years (she had not shot a film there since *The Peacemaker* by Mimi Leder, in 1997, and would not return there until 2003, for *The Stepford Wives*): 'For an actress, it's difficult, there are still not enough good female roles. It's an industry dominated by men. So I work around the world. I'm not interested in remaining in the United States.'[88]

The reactions of critics to *Moulin Rouge!* reflected the film itself: a kaleidoscope of excessive and contrasting reviews, provoked particularly by its Cannes premiere being accompanied by what was considered by some to be an over-lavish party. The post-screening celebration was so memorable that it caused Thierry Frémaux, the Festival's artistic director, to say, 'The future of the festival is Nicole Kidman, the star of the stars, both on the Croisette and, two hours later, dancing in the Moulin Rouge re-created on the harbour, surrounded by guests. This image is the symbol of the film festival.'[89] Critics also targeted the film's pyrotechnical appearance (while often ignoring its darker aspect), but they unanimously applauded Kidman's performance. In *Le Monde*, Samuel Blumenfeld wrote, 'Ewan McGregor makes prodigious efforts. Nicole, on the other hand, opts for a sobriety that is most welcome in a flashy film whose visual frenzy quickly makes one feel dizzy.'[90] Olivier Père expressed the same sentiments in *Les Inrockuptibles*: 'Baz Luhrmann persists in ugly kitsch and hysterical montage. But the pop classics and the sublime Nicole Kidman float above all this froth. [She is] contemporary American cinema's greatest and most beautiful actress. Her performance in *Moulin Rouge!* is as magnificent as in *To Die For* and *Eyes Wide Shut*, proving that a diamond will sparkle even in a plastic setting.'[91]

For Peck, in *Positif*, Kidman's beauty 'portrays here a superlative, magical state of the creature, in paradoxical contrast with the vulgarity

of the world that has created her, the cabaret ("the underworld"). A hybrid product of baroque, operatic theatricality and photogenic Hollywood. Even her nickname, "Sparkling Diamond", confirms the unreality of this apparition coated with a deadly glaze. It is a dematerialization created by the proliferation of weightless flight postures, the fetishizing cut of the costumes that sculpt a perfect body and the impenetrable web of finery in which the heroine is enmeshed.'[92] Finally, for Neil Smith, of the *BBC* website, 'it's Kidman who steals the movie with a devastating display of sultry allure. Watching her commit herself body and soul to Luhrmann's bizarre vision makes it easy to overlook the film's structural deficiencies and its tendency to sacrifice emotional resonance for stylistic bombast.'[93]

For other critics, the film's depiction of women raised questions. This was notably the case for Michael Charlton, who wrote, 'A problem with *Moulin Rouge!* as a postmodern film is that, while it attempts to mock melodrama […] it also attempts to recover melodrama. […] This attempt at genuine emotion relies on the deployment of a feminine stereotype which is not mocked – what might be described as the hooker with a heart of gold… While "Diamonds Are a Girl's Best Friend" parodies Hollywood femininity in its joking invocation of Monroe and Madonna and in the ironic self-awareness of Kidman as Satine, her sexualized role as "Sparkling Diamond" also attempts to set up a version of Satine that is not ironic… The postmodern star performance, which playfully references earlier icons, fails when the ironic detachment from those icons breaks down. Through the course of the film, Kidman arguably becomes Monroe (and Garbo and Dietrich…) merely repeating the gendered roles that they performed. The hyperbolic nature of the film paradoxically serves to underline the melodrama rather than subvert it.'[94]

Despite these mixed reviews, audiences worldwide voted in favour of *Moulin Rouge!* and, having started out with a budget of $50 million, the film brought in more than three times that amount at the box office. Moreover, most importantly, the star's glamorous image had become even more enhanced: Kidman had shown that she could act, sing and dance, and that she was also bankable throughout the world – despite the vehicle being a non-Hollywood production. She thus brought a new sparkle, a revitalized energy to cinematography outside of the United States film culture, in the company of British and Australian actors and writers. Luhrmann, who was also the film's producer, witnessed her emancipation: 'I felt a change happening to her. You see, she needs to get high emotionally. It's something that puts her at peace. It allows her to find something like flying in her work. And once she had got that, it was a release.'[95]

The return to her Australian homeland undoubtedly marks a turning-point in Kidman's filmography, signalling a rediscovered identity, a sort of rebalancing of the star's desires and perspectives. However, barely had Kidman recovered from her exhausting immersion than, like a modern Satine, she had to return to the shadows, this time in Spain, for a role with a more ghostly presence, in the morbid and claustrophobic horror film *The Others*.

When acting becomes reality. The character of Satine is undoubtedly one of the metaphorical and emotional peaks of Kidman's work.

# 6

# Grace Stewart

*The Others* (2001)
Alejandro Amenábar

'*The Others* was a scary time. I didn't like the way the story and the two children reflected my own situation.'[96]
Nicole Kidman, 2001

Kidman had finished *Moulin Rouge!* exhausted and her personal life was falling apart. Forced to go straight into *The Others*, co-produced by her husband Tom Cruise, she was unsettled: 'I was in a bad state, and I had to make that psychological journey [...] I wanted to drop out, and I tried to get Julianne Moore or Sharon Stone to come on board. I was having nightmares about it. But they said they would sue me. I kept telling them I did not want to do it. I was wilful and stubborn, but they said I had no choice.'[97] Overwhelmed, she joined the shoot in Spain, despite herself, but was finally won over by the talent of director Alejandro Amenábar, who also wrote the film's script and music. In fact, the young filmmaker was offering her the chance to tackle what for her was a new genre: the no-exit horror film. Moreover, in order to generate fear, the director intended to limit the use of special effects in favour of a greater intensity in the actors' performances. He explained: 'When you look at the situation of an actor in Hollywood today, you realize how pathetic it is. They're surrounded by special effects. I had at least to offer Nicole Kidman a written and complex role.'[98] The project in which Amenábar was keen to involve the actress was also an ambitious one: 'We spent a lot of time discussing her character's past. The film was located in England, we dyed Kidman's hair blond, I was obsessed with the idea of making a period film along the lines of *Rebecca*. Hence the research on the character's hairstyle. We became aware of the connection with Hitchcock only at the end of the second week of shooting. Nicole Kidman is a mixture of Vivien Leigh – her eyes – and Grace Kelly.'[99] The character played by Kidman is also called Grace, a recurring feature in her filmography: she later played Grace Mulligan for Lars von Trier, then Grace Kelly herself for Olivier Dahan. This name, often associated with gentleness and elegance, is synonymous with the religious concept of divine salvation, an idea that is particularly strong in *The Others*, a film with numerous religious references, which

notably bring into play the notions of hell, sin and redemption.

Grace Stewart, a lone mother, lives in a lugubrious mansion, in which she appears to be a prisoner. She proves to be powerless in the face of paranormal phenomena that are threatening the lives of her two children, who suffer from a strange illness: any exposure to light brighter than a candle would be fatal for them. Strange noises, doors that open by themselves, the unexplained disappearance of curtains: all conspire to undermine the young woman, who is struggling to maintain a strict and rational discipline, until the final revelation that calls into question our viewpoint on all these events. The film proposes multiple leads, putting Grace, as well as the viewers, to the test. We are led to doubt, successively, the new servants she has engaged and who seem to know a bit too much; their predecessors, who left without a trace; Anne (Alakina Mann), the insolent little girl who terrorizes her brother Nicholas (James Bentley) with ghost stories; and Grace herself, who oscillates between chilling intransigence and genuine anxiety.

Becoming Terror

In the prologue of *The Others*, Grace is at first a vibrating cord, a voice with a warm tone. This opening is a direct reference to the famous BBC radio series *Listen with Mother*, which ran from 1950 to 1982, and from which the film's first iconic phrase, 'Are you sitting comfortably?', is taken. But Grace does not whisper a beautiful story or a nursery rhyme, and the content of the story is particularly charged because Genesis is raised in several sentences, the young woman laying emphasis on divine omnipotence. Suddenly, in a brutal editing cut, we see a screaming woman facing the camera in a very cold, white light. This is Grace, who seems to have awoken from a horrible nightmare or to have given birth to a monster: perhaps to her own madness, her inconsolable solitude, her hallucinations, or even her latent violence, especially toward her children. This inaugural sequence is reminiscent of Pascal Quignard's *Petit Traité sur Méduse* (Little Treatise on Medusa): 'Why do women become mothers? They pass on the baton of that which horrifies

With *The Others*, Kidman tackles a no-exit horror film. She plays the role of Grace, a lone mother who lives in a lugubrious mansion, in which she appears to be a prisoner, with her children, Anne (Alakina Mann) and Nicholas (James Bentley).

Opposite and above: Grace is both a protective mother and a dangerous, profoundly troubled woman, beset by her own madness and her latent violence toward her children.

Following pages: Kidman, physically transformed since her performance in *Moulin Rouge!*, seems lost in the vastness of the big house.

them; they pass on the reflection of that which cannot be faced; they pass on a featureless front. They entrust the care of screaming to younger ones because they do not have the courage to take on hell alone… Women transfer the weight of death onto the backs of children that they bear in pain, their mouths wide open, screaming… Mothers pass on the scream.'[100] This break in tone plunges us directly into the essence of the film: a constant toing and froing between life and death, between a protective, loving mother and a dangerous, profoundly troubled woman.

This lead-in, conceived by the director, fits perfectly, like a sort of leitmotif, into Kidman's work as a whole. It is not unusual to see the actress waking up from bad dreams, notably in *Dead Calm* and *Eyes Wide Shut*, and she continues to play with the boundaries between truth and lies, dreams and reality, heaven and hell. David Thomson notes that 'Grace has had a dream that is, rather, the nightmare that the return of her husband, dead but full of accusations against her, would represent.' And, in relation to Kidman, he remarks, 'Her personification of hysteria (from this very first scene) is brilliant and unsettling.'[101]

Kidman's portrayal of awakening here is perhaps one of the most frightening of her career. Her face, pushed into a pillow, is distorted by the violence of the emotion: her veins stand out, her hands, pressed against her wide-open mouth,

tremble slightly, and her bulging eyes bring to mind the words of J. M. G. Le Clézio in *Mydriase*, his poetic work about the experiences induced by the use of recreational drugs: 'The eyes of the face were bombs constantly ready to explode.'[102] Even as Grace seems to be regaining her foothold on reality, her posture, sitting on the bed with her face tilted upward, reveals for a brief moment eyes rolled back into her head. This presentation of the character seems to place her from the outset as someone suffering deep pain, which erupts from her inner world at this point in an explosive cry. Portraying horror and conveying it to the audience also occurs via another facet of the character, perfectly mastered by Kidman, who effects a skilful mix between severity and childlike helplessness. For Grace must establish herself as the mistress of the house and keep order in the large mansion.

Kidman had transformed physically since her performance in *Moulin Rouge!* Thinner, she seems lost in the vastness of the big house and her face, which is very pale, seems longer. We notice, too, that her subtle make-up does not fill out her lips, as was the case with Satine or Suzanne Stone (*To Die For*), and her high, well-drawn eyebrows contrast with her white eyelids, widening her ever-watchful eyes. She thus seems particularly young and fragile, and often on the verge of tears. But when Grace is on form, she has a regal bearing, almost frightening in her perfectly fitted,

Opposite: Grace ceaselessly draws the curtains on the outside world, not so much to protect her children, to whom any exposure to light brighter than a candle would be fatal, as to safeguard herself from the cruel truth.

Following pages: Seeking to discover the origin of unexplained murmurs, the young woman finds herself alone in a room filled with furniture draped with dust covers. Seized by panic, she tears off the covers, one by one, searching for intruders, but discovers only her own reflection in a mirror.

austere clothing that reveals her obsession with control. Her exaggeratedly civilized manners are accompanied, however, by brittle, sharp movements. She sometimes displays a haughty, almost aristocratic air, and finishes her sentences with a hard, authoritative expression on her face when she explains that discipline and calm are very important to her.

The relationship with the three servants Grace has hired is thrown off balance by her attitude and forced smiles, which could be described as 'old school', like the acting style of film stars of the 1950s. However, Kidman manages to perfectly integrate these rather clichéd mannerisms. When, relieved, Grace joins her hands in prayer or, worried, puts her hand to her chest or presses her temples, these gestures, caught in the flow of movement, seem so sensitive and necessary that Kidman easily sidesteps the risk of an outdated performance. Grace's reactions to events also seem, at first sight, disproportionate in relation to those of the other characters. Mrs Mills (Fionnula Flanagan), the housekeeper, for example, remains perfectly calm, almost indifferent to the rebukes of the very agitated Grace, who has just found a door, which she had just shut, open. The panic-stricken young mother tries to establish her authority, which she believes has been flouted, by delivering orders in a shrill voice and in a tone that would be more suitable for reprimanding a child. Kidman manages to successfully portray the feeling of powerlessness of the character, who often gesticulates to no effect.

## Looking, Breathing, Feeling Isolated

Light being both a symbolic and a technical challenge of the film, *The Others* might be considered as a treatise about sight. At first, Grace does not want to see the limbo in which she is living, ceaselessly drawing the curtains on the outside world, not so much to protect her children as to safeguard herself from the cruel truth. Light presents a real test for the cinematography team since, in addition to changes in the set's general lighting, the always highly tricky issue of candlelight must be managed. In this respect, we must commend the work of Javier Aguirresarobe, who bathes the actors' faces in a modulated light in the style of Georges de La Tour. The lighting of Grace is often on the border between darkness and brightness, the demonic and the angelic. The brightness of her eyes is also particularly carefully rendered, which focuses the viewer's attention on those exaggerated eyes, which are desperate to see what they already know. Noteworthy in this respect is the sequence where Grace, who is seeking to discover the origin of unexplained murmurs, finds herself alone in a room filled with furniture draped with dust covers. Her eyes scan the room in all directions while the camera circles

around her. Growing increasingly wider, these eyes seem to be trying to see beyond the pristine whiteness of the sheets. Seized by an almost frenzied panic, Grace tears off the protective covers, one after the other, searching for intruders, but discovers only her own reflection in a mirror.

Here, Kidman rediscovers the primitive, fundamental dimension of the performance of screen actors in the early days of cinema, whose work was based essentially on gesture and the eyes. The question for Kidman is how to extend such an established use of eyes and expression in order to take us beyond the eyes, to the parallel, invisible world of the afterlife. Kidman's pupils, evoked in *Dead Calm*, seem to be made to (help us) see in the dark, in that which is beyond the visible, as described by Le Clézio: 'The eyes are looking, looking. They thrust their pale beams into the night, persistently, fiercely. They are going to see, they know it. They will look for so long that sight will appear. The gaze will manage to find that darkness.'[103] For Amenábar, Kidman possesses a 'gaze much more effective than any of the most sophisticated special effects'.[104] And what if she were more effective than any machine or form of artificial intelligence, a clairvoyant who could actually make us travel between worlds?

While developing her sickly performance in *Moulin Rouge!*, Kidman also worked on her breathing, her breaths emitted like a series of quavers and semiquavers. Any annoyance leads Grace to become short of breath, the clenching of her muscles seemingly causing her to fight for air. Each scene is thus an effort – even physically painful. We constantly feel her heart beating, the movements of her chest beneath her clothes betraying her mental agitation. Her whisperings are also augmented by the musical reverberations and the flute that weaves through the soundtrack. This is a performance that unfolds over time, hauntingly. In a way, Grace is more an echo than a real body, solitude personified, a mother abandoned by her husband and left to fend for herself in a huge house.

Kidman also knows how to give us an insight into Grace's great distress, while her many stunned expressions throughout the film represent blatant instances of humanity facing the unexpected and unfathomable. When Grace arrives at the gate of the house, following her husband who, after a brief return has left without a word, Kidman conveys with great sincerity her character's fatigue and despair confronted with this new abandonment. But she colours her expression with an unexpected trace of resignation, as though she were finally accepting her imprisonment. She presses her face between the two bars of the gate, forming an image that is highly symbolic of Kidman's position as an actress – a prisoner in a role she did not want to play, that of a mother herself imprisoned. While Grace has been in a state of nervous movement throughout

the film, running from door to door and from corridor to corridor, the final revelation leaves her stunned, at a standstill, petrified. At the end, with the look of a semi-lucid woman, tears in her eyes, she seems to be casting a spell on her children by asking them to repeat an incantation so that they remain with her. Grace has been neither a stereotypical mother nor a monstrous wife, a nuance that Kidman insisted on when in discussion with the director during shooting.

The young woman's gesticulations in the house reflect panic in the face of reason, and her body constantly assailed by horrific visions invites a sort of *danse macabre* with the unavoidable, all of which Kidman delivers with a sensitive and ambivalent dichotomy. This is exemplified by a scene in the film's final part, where Grace resolutely protects her children. At the same time, she encircles them stiffly, in a way that is both determined and frightening.

The Critics Play Along

With her personal life and media image on the rocks, Kidman preferred to focus on her involvement in *The Others* by talking about her way of seeing things: 'There's nothing worse than complacency. That terrifies me. Success can corrupt us. Getting to a certain level and then not feeling anything any more, no longer needing to put yourself to the test [...] That's terrible. Isn't it

all about risk-taking, well before worrying about the expectations of others? With each new role, you have to be free, forgetting how you played the earlier ones. Each time it's a new world.'[105] The press proved to be generally kind with regard to the film and her performance, noting of her fine audacity.

The *New York Times* critic played along: 'Ms. Kidman embodies [this role] with a conviction that is in itself terrifying. The icy reserve that sometimes stands in the way of her expressive gifts here becomes the foundation of her most emotionally layered performance to date... It's not every actress who can make a hard-headed rationalist like me believe in ghosts.'[106] The *Village Voice* had the same admiration for Kidman, highlighting the subtlety as well as the effectiveness of her performance: 'From beginning to end, Grace exists in a state of barely suppressed hysteria punctuated by moments of abject terror, all of which Kidman registers with extreme delicacy. We've seen her play this kind of trapped character before – most notably in *The Portrait of a Lady* – but not with such sustained, unnerved intensity. This is one scary movie, not because we see ghosts or monsters, but because Kidman makes us feel her fear as our own.'[107] Journalists endlessly analysed the secrets of her expressiveness, from the *San Francisco Chronicle* ('Nicole Kidman isn't the star of Alejandro Amenábar's *The Others*. Her skin is.

When Grace runs to the gate of the house, following her husband, who, after a brief return, has left without a word, Kidman conveys with great sincerity her character's fatigue and despair faced with this new abandonment.

Opposite: Kidman in *Bewitched* (2005) by Nora Ephron, the big-screen adaptation of the famous TV series of the 1960s.

Although other beautiful actresses have played witches – including recently Charlize Theron (*Snow White and the Huntsman*, 2012) and Angelina Jolie (*Maleficent,* 2014) – Kidman has repeated the experience more than once, to the extent that they have become a leitmotif in her career. Deeply affected in childhood by the witch in *The Wizard of Oz* (Victor Fleming, 1939), she has shown herself drawn to the evil or fantastical nature of these characters since the 1990s: in *To Die For* (1995), she played a criminal whose wide-brimmed hats gave her the air of a modern witch, then a friendly witch in *Practical Magic* (Griffin Dunne, 1998). Next, she played a ghost in *The Others* (2001), a manipulative monster in *The Golden Compass* (Chris Weitz, 2007), a nymphomaniac willing to heal the wounds of a young boy by urinating on him in *The Paperboy* (Lee Daniels, 2012) and a taxidermist who will stop at nothing in *Paddington* (Paul King, 2014). One of the main qualities of Kidman's portrayal of witches is that she often plays on her fair complexion and her serenity, and needs neither make-up nor gothic costume to assume the role. Her witches, furthermore, are not all bad; they are nuanced and sometimes even positive. In all of these roles, Kidman enjoys maintaining the confusion between good and evil, and reflecting on the representation of women in society. It is therefore almost natural to see the actress portray the best-known TV witch of the twentieth century – the heroine of the series *Bewitched* – in the eponymous film by Nora Ephron, released in 2005. Incidentally, this meeting did not fail to escape commentators of the time: 'You don't need to read Michelet [*Satanism and Witchcraft*, published in French as *La Sorcière*, 1862] from start to finish to understand that the cultural perception of witchcraft always involves the circumstantial idea that a society has of women. Before *Bewitched* the series, this myth had insinuated itself in suburban 1960s America, questioning its dreams of domestic bliss and ordinary happiness… Who better than Kidman to play a woman embarrassed by her superiority over humans and sometimes full of empathy for their miserable state? Such was already the case in *Dogville*… everything about her is so strange that the emptiest of shots of her face is like a spell.'[i]

Has it ever been paler or clammier-looking? Her flesh is part of the mise-en-scene.')[108] to *L'Express* ('Fear whispers in exchanged glances. It is birthed in Nicole Kidman's eyes, spreads to those she looks at. They, in turn, pass it on to the other characters, who exchange knowing looks… Nicole Kidman becomes the flesh of this mansion.')[109] Her voice, 'a very effective instrument of expressive amplification' is also celebrated by *Positif*: 'The variations, both in intensity and tone, and register shifts determine or modify a climate, an atmosphere, an emotional tonality: the hushed voice, the toneless whispering match the obsession for silence and semi-darkness, then authoritarian outbursts add sudden explosions. Nicole Kidman's slender thread of a voice swells suddenly, ominously altering her personality. The change of intonation within the same scene indicates the simultaneous presence of contradictory impulses, thus birthing dread (it's the film's *Psycho* aspect).'[110]

In the end, *The Others* was a spectacular success worldwide (gaining huge returns for a $17 million budget), became Spanish cinema's biggest commercial hit and won many awards – notably seven Goyas (Spain's main national film award) – while Kidman was also nominated a Golden Globe for Best Actress. The actress, who was avoiding the press as much as possible, quickly embarked on another project. Finding refuge in England, she got under the skin

and into the soul of Virginia Woolf. The painful and spectral experience of *The Others* had certainly prepared her for such a role.

In *The Others*, Kidman's acting style resembles that of film stars of the 1950s. But caught in the flow of the moment, her rather clichéd mannerisms seem so sensitive and necessary that she sidesteps the risk of delivering an outdated performance.

Opposite: Grace's face often borders darkness and light, the demonic and the angelic.

# 7

# Virginia Woolf

*The Hours* (2002)
Stephen Daldry

'I was deeply depressed at that time, with thoughts of suicide.'[111]
Nicole Kidman, 2012

Kidman initially turned down the role of Virginia Woolf: 'For me, it was a casting error; it was impossible to be this icon of English literature, [but] Stephen Daldry believed in me and that's very appealing! The director is a painter and I'm just one of the colours on his palette. Some actors want to control everything, from the production to the writing via the direction; that's not the case with me.'[112] Adapted by David Hare from the eponymous novel (1998) by Michael Cunningham, *The Hours* portrays three women of different periods, all linked by mental illness, their relationships with Virginia Woolf's novel *Mrs Dalloway* (1925) and its main character. This trio are Woolf herself (Nicole Kidman) in the 1920s; Laura Brown (Julianne Moore), who, in the sanitized 1950s America, is trying to overcome her angst and is encouraged to change her life by the character Mrs Dalloway, with whom she identifies; and Clarissa Vaughan (Meryl Streep), who, in the present day, is caring for Laura's son, Richard Brown (Ed Harris), a writer with AIDS. He is suicidal and nicknames his friend 'Mrs Dalloway'. The spectre of Woolf pervades the lives of each character. As Laure Becdelièvre elaborates: 'all the film's symbols and images serve this aim: in the quiet hours, in a riverbed, lingering in the furnishings, nestles sometimes depression, sometimes visual beauty, sometimes ambiguous desire, sometimes morbid obsession. All human traces left by bodies who on screen embody the multiple facets of a single soul.'[113]

Kidman joined the filming in the house that was once Woolf's home (in Richmond, Surrey, west of central London), which inspired her: 'We rehearsed in this house; we spent a lot of time in this house, which is always beneficial; far better than rehearsing in a rehearsal room, because you have the presence and the environment and you feed off that. You feed off so many things as an actor. You're never quite sure of what's going to be your trigger. It can be a dress or the way you just walk down the stairs or the colour of the walls. Ann Roth is one of our greatest costume designers and an extraordinary woman [...] She gave that dress, which was suddenly so Virginia.'[114]

From the day the cameras started rolling, everyone was wondering where Kidman had disappeared to, as she was unrecognizable thanks to the work of make-up artist Paul Engelen, wigmaker Peter Owen, optician Mitchell Cassel (who made her wear contact lenses) and the GA Enterprises agency (who created her special false teeth). Finally, a prosthetic nose transformed her face and completely reinvented her. Even the paparazzi, who were stalking her during the shoot, were not able to spot her (she deliberately went out into the road without removing the prosthesis). Kidman, who on set rolled her own cigarettes (just as did Woolf), recalls, 'I threw myself headlong into the character of Virginia Woolf, changing my way of speaking, walking, writing. But I don't want everything to be about my nose! Talking for an hour about this appendage is missing the point. It would be to reduce everything to an artifice when it was not about that; I experienced a metamorphosis to the very depths of my being.'[115] Kidman immersed herself in the writer's letters and trained herself to write with her right hand (she is left-handed), even learning to copy Woolf's handwriting. Physically and spiritually, she got right to the heart of this giant of literature, and fell in love with an artist whose torments she intimately shared at the time.

## Kidman and Woolf

The cultural convergence of the Australian actress and the British novelist is the more surprising in that it was not planned: Kidman was not at all familiar with Woolf's work. 'My knowledge of English literature, I admit, was confined to the novels of the Brontë sisters, George Eliot and the Romantics Byron and Shelley. Discovering Virginia Woolf in my thirties was a unique experience. She had a great power of fascination and attraction over me. I literally fell in love with her... I think she was an extraordinary person. She had a beautiful spirit, intelligence and genius. She embraced life in all its complexity.'[116] The actress found in the writer's words and suffering a striking, dazzling echo of her own shattered life: '[Virginia Woolf] wrestled with death, illness and love. Her life was a constant struggle. The tragic nature of her life makes her fascinating. But that's not all she was; there was also in her a sense

Kidman, who plays the writer Virginia Woolf, recalls that she 'threw herself headlong into the character, changing [her] way of speaking, walking, writing', and deplored the fact that what most people remember was the prosthetic nose she wore in the film.

of mischief, a playfulness and a *joie de vivre* that attracted others. Unfortunately, it was her other side that won out.'[117]

By her own admission, Kidman could recount, frame by frame, the station scene in *The Hours*: Virginia flees from the house, but her husband tries to convince her not to leave. The actress recalls, 'I can remember word for word what she said at that moment: "I'm living in a town I have no wish to live in. I'm living a life I have no wish to live." I remember them because never had the words placed in the mouth of one of my characters seemed more to belong to me.'[118] Who better than a depressed artist to play Woolf? During shooting, when the star walks, fully clothed, into an icy river to accompany her character to the other world, like an Ophelia, she is in a trance, in a wild, almost de-civilized state. For Becdelièvre, 'in immersing herself in the Ouse, dignified and determined, Virginia Woolf is not simply carrying out a premeditated suicide; she is slipping into both the time and hours that are floating by; into psychological life and its fluctuations; into death, which at times claims to be rejuvenation, at others freedom; into femininity, which provokes introspection; into motherhood, which worries; into writing and reading, which *The Hours*… invites us to experience fully, like an immersion; and into the very essence of cinema, which finds in water a vital motif.'[119] We wonder what Woolf would have felt seeing herself portrayed in this way, having in 1926 (a year after the publication of *Mrs Dalloway*) written about the marvels of cinema: 'People say that the savage no longer exists in us, that we are at the fag-end of civilization, that everything has been said already, and that it is too late to be ambitious. But these philosophers have presumably forgotten the movies… And sometimes at the cinema in the midst of its immense dexterity and enormous technical proficiency, the curtain parts and we behold, far off, some unknown and unexpected beauty.'[120]

## (Re)Incarnation(s)

*The Hours* begins with an unidentified subject: a rather awkward gait, a stooped, twisted silhouette. It is impossible to recognize a Hollywood star in this woman, with her piercing gaze and witch-like nose. 'In short, by means of her "false nose",' as Becdelièvre emphasizes, 'Nicole Kidman, alias Virginia Woolf, assumes a general unease. This "evil in being two" – which Friedrich Nietzsche and Stéphane Mallarmé had also put in words and verse a few years before the English author – opens the way at the same time to a salvation, a gratification through poetry.'[121]

Admittedly, the art of make-up is, as the philosopher and sociologist Edgar Morin states,

'the successor of the masks and the doll-like make-up of Ancient Greece and Eastern civilizations'.[122] He notes that make-up 'de-personalizes' the face and 'gives it a new eloquence. It de-personalizes the star in order to over-personalize her.'[123] Yet it was less a matter here for Kidman to 'over-personalize' herself, than to enter into the character to such an extent that she loses herself. Essentially, she does not really resemble Woolf, as the British author David Thomson points out,[124] but rather Princess Anne, Lady Diana or Charlotte Brontë. Above all, she seems to be seeking to live down a well-known face rather than attempt a futile imitation. She gives the character a hollow voice, as though she had come back from the dead. Her hands, old and skeletal, tremble. She plays with her hands and her pen, which seem to be constantly in suspension: she holds her cigarette in the air and her whole body seems precisely suspended from her inner world. Kidman attempts a personal reincarnation of the writer's body and of her dark and radiant ideas.

Often despondent and fidgeting with her hands, Woolf does not know what to do with her body. Kidman plays a woman who is absorbed, distraught, in the limbo of a parallel universe, in which she is searching for inspiration. This dimension is one of the main attractions for the actress: 'I love the idea of searching for somebody and coming up with an idea. How do you write?

When do things hit you? As an actor, things hit me at the strangest times. Suddenly, I'll say, Oh, I must not forget this, etc. When do you become inspired? That was something that was really fun to work on and somehow try to generate the energy and the ideas that allow them to exist in the head. Stephen Daldry gave me a direction; he said, "Think of it like electricity." When the idea finally hits and goes down your arm, into your hand, through your fingers, into the pen and onto the paper. Rapidly. That was very, very beneficial having that image.'[125]

Virginia is asked several times whether she is there, what she is thinking, but, as her sister Vanessa (Miranda Richardson) explains, the writer really has two lives: the one she is living and the book that she is writing. Kidman masters her expression of Woolf's gaze perfectly ('The eyes are fierce, angry, bitter over time or calm, lost'[126]) and manages to differentiate several states of consciousness between objective reality and her character's imaginary projections. When Virginia is sitting on a bench, she seems rather tall in comparison, making her seem like an otherworldly creature, giant and hunched over, next to her straight-backed, well-arranged sister. Wearing a dress that is more work smock than woman's dress, and too big for her, Virginia floats in her clothes, like a ghost. With her right hand in her pocket, her gauche, almost masculine posture and her hat pulled down over her eyes, Kidman's

In playing Virginia Woolf, the actress seems, above all, to be seeking to live down a well-known face rather than attempt a futile imitation.

Opposite: When she is sitting on a bench with her sister (Miranda Richardson), Virginia seems like a giant, floating in her clothes, like a ghost.

Virginia is plain, unkempt and looks almost ill, like Richard Brown, the other poet in the film.

The creators portrayed in *The Hours* are mad and fragile, their lifeblood sucked from them by their intensive labouring. Kidman depicts this decomposition, which is like a flower fading. While epochs intermingle on the screen, accompanied by Philip Glass's cyclic music, she moulds time, measuring silences and micro-spaces. This is particularly evident when Virginia is with her young niece, with whom she reflects on the mysteries of death. The young woman's face is constantly tense, whether she is frowning or raising her eyebrows, confessing her ignorance to the child. This facial invariability reflects a permanent tension in the character as a whole, whose movements are as stiff and hesitant when she is laying flowers next to a dead bird. Her body does not seem consistent with the fluidity and vivacity of the ideas that scroll through her mind. Her eyes, which appear huge, seem to dive into this other world, recalling in a way Grace Stewart's fixed gaze at the end of *The Others*.

Kidman manages, in an unprecedented way, to portray the intricacies of this deeply creative and tortured inner world. When Virginia expresses her annoyance with her imposed confinement in her house, the actress intentionally accentuates her pronunciation of the word 'obligation'. The writer yearns for emotional and artistic freedom. Infuriated by her husband,

who is wanting only to protect her but who she feels is oppressing her, she is at the end of her resources, finishing her sentences with a strained exhalation, which betrays her anguish. Her emphases and her delivery, which accelerates suddenly, highlight her extreme agitation. So it is a whole ghost-like body that trembles, seethes and is reborn in this suffering. Her eyes, which again gaze with unusual intensity, convey a multitude of feelings generated by Virginia's angst.

Having performed all these demanding, transcendent scenes where the character takes on the physicality of a ghost, Kidman avoids theorizing about or intellectualizing her way of working: 'I really try not to talk. When you start to dissect a performance, you take away the mystery. I think there is too much talk about how it's done, it's far better to allow it to exist as a piece of work and in the story. These days there is too much information.'[127]

## A Crowning Achievement

The critics were so impressed by Kidman's performance that they had fun questioning whether it really was the Australian actress who had taken on the guise of the British writer. At the 2003 Berlin International Film Festival, where the film was one of the Festival's picks and Kidman, Meryl Streep and Julianne Moore jointly won Silver Bear for Best Actress, *Libération*

Opposite and above:
Kidman plays a woman
who is absorbed,
often despondent, lost in the
limbo of a parallel universe.

Following pages: The actress
moulds time, measuring
silences and micro-spaces,
particularly when she reflects
on the mysteries of death
with her young niece,
Angelica (Sophie Wyburd).

reports, 'The film tells us clearly that it is Virginia Woolf. Yes, but this actress, beneath the writer's name? The credits assure us that it is Nicole Kidman, and yet this is hard to believe: physically unrecognizable, but above all transfigured by her performance, beyond sensational. This distortion is not some empty gimmick; rather it expresses the subtlety of a screenplay that is constantly confronting the geometry of space and time.'[128] Similarly, *Le Nouvel Obs* enthuses, 'The actress is unrecognizable, to the point where we come to doubt that we have correctly read the credits. A *tour de force*, yes, on the part of the make-up artists as well as the actress. The vanity of actors sometimes lies in their desire to hide, to disappear, or rather to pretend. Nicole Kidman, however, does not pretend, nor does she hide – instead she applies herself to being. To being Virginia Woolf…. It is in this that her creation is so admirable; the achievement of the make-up artists serves only to reflect the totally internalized performance of the actress, who becomes a woman of the past and, even more essentially, becomes the writer.'[129] For *France Soir*, 'Nicole Kidman marvellously reproduces her turbulent internal turmoil and the somnambulistic wanderings of a living woman who is already dead… Since her divorce from Tom Cruise, the actress's image has changed. No one could any longer see in her the awkward and giggling figure who used to follow

her husband like his shadow. It is now Kidman who is overshadowing Cruise; she can be considered a Hollywood superstar doubled with a versatile actress who remains unruffled whatever the challenge.'[130]

On the other side of the Atlantic, too, it was time for admiration: 'Nicole Kidman de-glams herself with a fake nose to play suicidal author Virginia Woolf, but there's nothing fake about her performance.'[131] *The New York Times* extolled Kidman's inner power: 'Directing her desperate, furious stare into the void, her eyes not really focusing, Ms. Kidman, in a performance of astounding bravery, evokes the savage inner war waged by a brilliant mind against a system of faulty wiring that transmits a searing, crazy static into her brain.'[132] Academics, on the other hand, were divided by the star's transformation. The Canadian researcher Martha Musgrove confessed to having been irritated by the prosthesis: 'What really put me off was The Nose. Nicole Kidman wore a permanent frown and looked cross-eyed throughout the film, clearly distressed at this Thing in the middle of her face. Were Woolf's contemporaries preoccupied with her nose? It never really occurred to me that her proboscis was the defining feature, so to speak, of Woolf's appearance.'[133] Similarly, according to Woolf authority Brenda R. Silver, this portrayal of the novelist is not really credible: 'In her lifetime Woolf was considered to have come from a family

Winner of several awards during the early years of her career in Australia, Kidman has since received spectacular recognition for her work in the United States and Europe. In 1992, her performance in *Billy Bathgate* (Robert Benton, 1991) brought her first Golden Globe nomination, an award which, to date, she has won three times, for *To Die For* in 1996, *Moulin Rouge!* in 2002 and *The Hours* in 2003, a particularly auspicious year. At a time when her personal life was in crisis, Kidman also won an Oscar, a BAFTA and the Berlin Silver Bear for *The Hours* as well as a star on the Hollywood Walk of Fame. Among the other honours that have marked her career, she was named as a member of the jury at the Cannes Film Festival in 2012, an event to which she has often been invited. All these marks of respect are important to the actress, who has long sought the approval and pride of her parents, although they would doubtless have preferred their daughter to become a great reporter or scientist and to win the Nobel Prize, an award that is more important in their eyes than the sparkle of showbiz.

For her, however, these rewards remain institutional victories similar to a university degree, which she lacks, the recognition of a level of commitment, a level of excellence, which no doubt accounts for her deliberately politicized speech when she received her Oscar, in her parents' presence. During the staid ceremony, unaccustomed to political receptions, Kidman drew a parallel between the victims of 9/11 and those of the war in the Middle East, before millions of viewers (the US invasion of Iraq had begun earlier that very same week). These international honours have clearly given her wings and she has gradually got involved with humanitarian and intergovernmental organizations, notably the United Nations, who appointed her UN Women's Goodwill Ambassador in 2006. Like other actresses, Kidman uses her celebrity to support causes and raise funds, but also tries, privately, to honour her family's feminist and pacifist commitments.

Opposite: Nicole Kidman
at the unveiling of her star
on Hollywood's *Walk of Fame*,
13 January 2003.

Kidman's Virginia Woolf plays
with her hands, which seem
to be constantly in suspension.
Indeed, her whole body seems
precisely suspended from
her inner world.

Following pages: The actress
and her director, Stephen
Daldry, share a light-hearted
moment during the shoot.

of great beauties. Her photograph appeared
in *Vogue* London and the British photographer
Cecil Beaton included her portrait in his 1930
*Book of Beauty*, writing of her "chaste and
somber beauty".' Silver added that 'It was a
mistake to make her so dowdy', arguing that
the dowdiness feeds into the 'belief that
intellectual women aren't stylish or fashionable or
beautiful.'[134] Despite these few dampers, Kidman
collected several awards, including an Oscar for
Best Actress, and audiences were equally generous
with their praise: *The Hours* grossed more
than $100 million at the box office (four times
its budget), an unexpected success for an intimate
period drama.

Exhausted, Kidman sensed it was time
to take a career break. She made the most of it,
using the several months to read and to recharge
her batteries; she confessed, 'I credit books
with me becoming an actor. Because it was how
I originally would absorb a character. I couldn't
wait, when I was eleven, to pick up a novel
and just disappear into it. And I was devastated
when it ended.'[135] But, completely involved
in her career, she soon returned to the front line:
as she plainly stated, 'Being an actress isn't
a choice, but a vital necessity. It's in my blood.
Although my way of working changes from
one role to another, I love, in general, to be
consumed, to get passionately involved and lose
myself.'[136] And, indeed, she once again threw

herself into working on roles for accomplished
directors Anthony Minghella (*Cold Mountain*),
Robert Benton (*The Human Stain*) and,
controversially, Lars von Trier, for whom,
in *Dogville*, she consciously endangered her now
institutionalized star status.

# 8

# Grace Margaret Mulligan

*Dogville* (2003)
Lars von Trier

'The important thing for me was knowing that [Lars von Trier] had written the film for me. We've had a very close and very complicated relationship. He can be very gentle or very […] complicated. I don't know where I am with him, I never know, but now I'm dependent.'[137]
Nicole Kidman, 2003

Although at the height of her fame in Hollywood, having been awarded the Oscar for Best Actress (for *The Hours*), Kidman decided to leave for a remote suburb in Northern Europe in order to make a film in a desolate warehouse, under the direction of a Danish filmmaker with a scandalous reputation. For Lars von Trier this was also a gamble: 'Nicole wanted to make the film, whereas Björk [in his *Dancer in the Dark*, 2000] had wanted to survive the experience. That makes a huge difference on set! [Nicole] wanted to work with me, so I wrote the part of Grace for her, without really knowing her. I had only seen her in *Eyes Wide Shut*.'[138] The film depicts the behaviour of the inhabitants of Dogville, who are upset by the arrival of a mysterious young woman fleeing from hostile authorities as well as threats from gangsters. The small town will allow her to stay only on condition that she performs the chores set for her daily by its residents. This willing servitude, taken to the extreme, is organized into a prologue and nine chapters.

Working with von Trier

Accepting what was a pittance of a fee, given her status as an international star, Kidman explained her desire to venture into a disturbed world that was new to her: 'I chose to do *Dogville* because at the time I was getting offered these big American comedies; I had done *Moulin Rouge!*, I had done *The Others*, I had done things that I call large films, and I wanted to go and work with Lars on something very, very small because I am a huge believer in supporting the auteurs that are not necessarily financially viable. I liked the Brechtian qualities of the script and I liked how he was challenging the ideas of how we treat other human beings and what are our agendas and deep motives behind these desires to help.'[139] Regarding the character of Grace, she confessed, 'I think I just connected with her implicitly. There was

something about the way she tries to help this community and her desire to be of service and to help; that was the way in which I could connect with her.'[140]

For his part, the filmmaker admitted, 'I was already thinking about *Dogville*, but I was envisaging a much tougher, darker heroine. As soon as Nicole got involved with the project, she made me soften the character of Grace, because she herself is gentle. I think she's a good person: having everything she's got – beauty, talent, fortune, success – is quite dangerous. But she copes with it well. Perhaps her Australian roots give her a solid foundation, a healthy core. I like these descendants of British convicts. In any case, it occurred to me, while preparing the film, that a woman like her is perhaps a troublesome gift for the small village community.'[141]

As she had on the shoot of *Eyes Wide Shut*, Kidman discovered an intense way of working: 'It was a challenge to do it, because there were no walls and there were a few props but not much; it was also very, very freeing and very liberating.'[142] She explained von Trier's method: 'He holds the camera himself and while we're shooting he is talking to the actors. You have to arrive at a state where you can hear his voice without letting it distract you.'[143] For von Trier, it meant being 'as near to the actors as possible. Often I'll move a hand or adjust a piece of clothing, or ask a question without stopping the take. The advantage of the video camera is that you can shoot for hours without interruption. I don't cut between takes; we shoot a scene, start again, the camera records everything; it's like a game.'[144] For once, he shot scenes in the chronological order of the story, which enabled the actress to control the narrative crescendo of the film via the progressive intensity of her performance. Shooting lasted six weeks and editing took nine months.

However, it was this sense of claustrophobic adventure that, above all, left a lasting impression on Kidman: 'Lars can ask you to do strange things. You can't allow yourself to be intimidated and need to look him straight in the eye and say "No", "Shut up", or even "But what are you doing naked on set? Go and get dressed, it's more sensible." Then he calms down and comes back down to earth.'[145] Perhaps Kidman was

Previous pages:
The minimalist setting
in which the characters
in the story evolve is rooted
in the Great Depression.

Opposite, top: Grace
(Nicole Kidman) with Gloria
(Harriet Andersson) and Ma
Ginger (Lauren Bacall),
the shopkeeper who gives
her a chance.

Opposite, bottom: The young
woman befriends Jack McKay
(Ben Gazzara), who lives as a
recluse and refuses to admit
that he is blind.

Above: Having convinced
the residents of Dogville
to hide Grace, who is being
pursued by gangsters, Tom
(Paul Bettany), an indecisive
writer, becomes infatuated
with the stranger.

Following pages: Chuck
(Stellan Skarsgård), whose
children Grace looks after,
finally opens up to her.

rediscovering in the anarchic and politically aware
spirit of the filmmaker the sense of rebellion that
permeated her own family. In her youth, she used
to distribute 'very left-wing' tracts for her father.
'My parents were unconventional. Today, I'm very
grateful to them for that', she recalls.[146] Von Trier,
in return, was amazed by the actress: 'I have a
great deal of admiration for Nicole. She has dared
to do things that I didn't believe she was capable
of. *Dogville* is a film in which you could easily lose
yourself. Nicole never lost herself; she even found
great freedom of expression in it. It was exciting
to take a Hollywood star and put her in a project
like this one. She trusted me completely and for
that I'm very grateful to her. Nicole is an
intelligent actress who, I believe, doesn't define
herself in terms of success and dollars.'[147]

## The Total Commodity–Star

Is *Dogville*, with its unique scenic plan (walls are
represented by lines drawn on the ground), a film
about the acting profession? The microcosm it
depicts recalls a film set, behind the scenes, where
physical promiscuity affects the minds of the
actors and gradually disturbs their behaviour,
leading to frustration, paranoia and humiliation,
which also infects their relationships with the
stars of the show. As Louis Guichard wrote, 'In
parachuting Nicole Kidman into a Scandinavian
troupe, the director apparently had a brilliant

idea, and gave another "meta-meaning" to his
story: the star who descended from the
Hollywood heavens to the foreign filmmaker's
movie garden, etc. Yet, it is much more
complicated than that: in this film Kidman joins
Lauren Bacall, as well as James Caan and Ben
Gazzara, Chloë Sevigny and Stellan Skarsgård
(a favourite actor of the director's), and even
Harriet Andersson, who was Bergman's Monika
[…] The star can not therefore rely on the contrast
of her presence with others to portray the enigma
that is Grace.'[148] It is inevitable that we perceive
*Dogville* as a reflection on actors and film stars,
particularly in this theatrical space that resembles
a rehearsal room. But this dimension is not alone
in reflecting Kidman's relation to the film. There
is also the manner in which, during the course of
the story, her status changes from that of human
being to that of commodity for the inhabitants
of Dogville.

If, as Peter Baechlin noted, 'the lifestyle of stars
is itself a commodity',[149] these stars are also,
according to Edgar Morin, 'a total commodity…
There is not an inch of [their] body, not a fibre
of [their] soul, not a memory of [their] life that
cannot be thrown onto the market… Star-goddess
and star-commodity are the two sides of the same
reality.'[150] In *Dogville*, everything conspires to
topple Kidman the star from her pedestal in order
to transform her into a common commodity
(Grace ends up being raped by all the men

in the village). From the beginning, the unusual set is filmed using flattened high-angle shots with no perspective, providing no way out. This panoptic view inevitably recalls Michel Foucault's notion of the all-seeing eye in his book *Discipline and Punishment*, in which he analyses 'the body of the condemned', 'the spectacle of the scaffold', 'generalized punishment', 'docile bodies' and 'the means of correct training'.[151] This is exactly what is in store for Grace.

She first appears as a movie shadow, a long, tall silhouette, to the word 'illustration' spoken in the voice-over. In the flickering light, she emerges as if from the thoughts of the writer Tom Edison (Paul Bettany), whose name is a reference to one of the inventors of electrical lighting and the movie camera. Her first appearance, like a hunched phantom, is also somewhat menacing as it occurs at night. Grace is wearing a fur-collared coat, which gives her the air of a vulture or of a Hollywood star turning up among common folk. Kidman – who as an actress is an expert in portraying duplicity and many layers of meaning, at the opposite end of the scale from transparency – is plunged into a world without walls, where people and their jobs are labelled. In other words, a world that represents everything she is not.

In any case, Kidman is, by way of her character, being given an acting assignment once more: Grace has two weeks to ingratiate herself with the citizens of Dogville, to merge into the role she is being forced to assume. It is a matter of survival: she must play the game in order to avoid capture from those she is fleeing. The young woman's determination and charm gradually begin to have an effect. She proves to be particularly conciliatory and humble, using diplomacy to gain people's acceptance. Kidman's performance perfectly reflects Grace's character. She speaks softly, keeping her smile in all circumstances. Her gestures are gentle, both discreet and attentive, emphasizing the submissive attitude she has willingly adopted. Required to work for strangers for an hour a day per household, Grace casts off her fine clothing and soon looks like a housewife. She has been de-personalized, divested of her goddess-like status. She is compared to Miss Laura, a prostitute. Many mythological figures are then alluded to, in particular that of the Trojan Horse, Grace's integration being seen as a test for community. She becomes everything and anything, combining all roles, assuming all duties, which suits the townspeople perfectly, at least initially.

A Platonic Figure

Things go awry when Grace tries to open their eyes. She then becomes a Platonic grain of sand in a cave of ignorance: 'grace, divine light, exterior to the cave, the light of exteriority, independent of the closed, controlled system, of a world

Grace in one of the rare dreamlike sequences in the film.

Opposite: Kidman and von Trier on set. The actress had planned to resume her role as Grace in another film by the director, *Manderlay* (2004), but it was finally shot without her.

Following pages: Tom receives the stranger into his house the night of her arrival.

Extract from 'Nicole and Me', by Lars von Trier, in *Les Inrockuptibles*, 14 May 2003.

'It wasn't I who contacted Nicole Kidman, but she who first expressed a desire to work with me. When I read that in a magazine, I had never seen a film she'd been in. Then I watched *Eyes Wide Shut* by Stanley Kubrick, in which I found her fantastic, much more interesting than Tom Cruise, particularly in the scene with the joint, where she is truly remarkable. She is an excellent actress, notably because she is very hard working, very disciplined. She is also brave and bold and attempts difficult films. *Dogville* is very different from what she had done before and I have the impression that she really loved that. She trusted me completely, which is fundamental between an actor and a director, and which was a novelty for me after Björk. We had discussions, points of disagreement, but it was always to improve the film, never about anything other than the work. Nicole Kidman allowed me to make lots of mistakes, which is very important, because that's how you progress. My work requires that the actors make mistakes so that the film looks real. She always wanted to work more, to try a particular take in a particular way, and so on. That's really inspiring for a filmmaker. The only relationship problem that I had to deal with during the shoot did not concern Nicole Kidman, but the fact that we had a large group of actors confined in the same place for six weeks.'

of signs arranged by a director', as Alexandre Georgandas explained.[152] The character is a bearer of both truths and pretences, for she herself is a show, an image. She monopolizes the men's gazes, but they are all afraid of her picture, which is shown on a missing person's appeal (the word 'missing' on the poster symbolizes loss, absence and the search for a missing body and soul). Later, a new poster is put up. More than a quest for a lost object or animal, this time the poster launches a (wo)manhunt (the word 'wanted' is spelled out) in the spirit of an American western. Grace is named as an outlaw.

To offset the increased risk for the residents of Dogville, who are in trouble with the authorities, it is decided that Grace should work harder and for less pay. She is thus told to produce more and to show up more often, twice a day, in each household. Accelerated by the film's edit, Grace becomes an automaton; she is dehumanized. With a scarf on her head, she looks like a rag doll, or one of the workers in *Dancer in the Dark*, a second-class citizen. Her body is no longer her own. Grace adopts a diplomatic attitude fitting for a star who does not want to create controversy, who is looking for permanent consensus. Wanting to avoid offending the crowd at all costs, she accepts the inhabitants' wishes and excuses all their weaknesses. But they want ever more and demand physical touch from her. Jason (Miles Purinton), the son of Chuck (Stellan Skarsgård) and Vera (Patricia Clarkson), blackmails her perversely, demanding to be spanked. Uncomfortable with the pressure the child is putting on her, she tries to reason with and reassure him, but ends up doing it. She seems tense and raises her voice for the first time. Kidman manages to portray the distress of the young woman, who suddenly loses her composure and hurries her movements, as distraught by the boy's attitude as she is by what she has just done. In a complete denial of reality, Grace is made to pay for her image status. And the violence escalates as the actress's performance becomes increasingly internalized.

Kidman, who journeys a long way into masochism here, recalls, 'Probably the most challenging scene in *Dogville* was when he put the collar around my neck. I hated it and it was terrible because when they put it on me and I had to do the choking scene and I had to start choking because it was too tight, it actually was too tight at one point and it was pulling and I couldn't breathe, but because I'm choking in the scene, everyone thought I was just acting, and when they finally called cut I said "get this off me, get this off me" I couldn't speak, and then they realized what was actually happening. So what you see in the film was actually what happened, and it was terrifying.'[153] One of the most representative scenes of Kidman's performance is that where Vera, in an act of vengeance, smashes Grace's

figurines in front of her. For Grace, these small children's toys are all that remains of humanity. Turning back on the lessons in stoicism that she has been teaching her children, Vera intends to test Grace's ability to control her emotions, like an actress. Grace, who herself has become porcelain-like and silent, suffers real mental torture and breaks down sobbing. Kidman, always serious in her intention, lets us see the terrible thoughts that must be churning around in Grace's mind and the pressure of all these traumas. After this outburst, Grace falls into an attitude of profound indifference. Kidman, imperturbable, makes sure never to express anything from this point onwards – the ultimate challenge of the performance.

In the final twist, where Grace's father, a mob boss, comes to retrieve his daughter, all that remains of the character is this dreadful self-control. Her expression seems lost; she seems sometimes dazed and adopts a rather haughty air. For we understand that Grace has formed a firm conviction. She excuses the criminals, who, in her eyes, were only obeying their nature. She gets into the wide black car, which looks like a hearse or an actor trailer, and agrees to the curtains being open so that she can watch, in her turn, her father's gangsters destroying the village and killing its inhabitants. The image has turned against her public. There remains only the star, simultaneously angelic and malefic. Grace was indeed a Trojan Horse.

Critical Echoes

When asked to describe in a few words her experience acting in *Dogville*, Kidman replied, 'deep, provocative, emotional, challenging, liberating, intoxicating, and bizarre'.[154] She was as precise in the appraisal she gave of her collaboration with von Trier: 'I think working with Lars changes the way you think about society. He challenges you on everything. We used to go hiking in the snow together and drive around in his little camper van and he would challenge me on my religion, my philosophies, my ideas about life, and I think that's good. I think the conflict at times works because he stirs things up. The thing about Lars, though, is he is trying to find something authentic, he is always digging, digging, digging because he wants to find something in you that no one else has found.'[155]

The film was in competition for the Palme d'Or at the 2003 Cannes Film Festival, where, at the press conference, the director had to answer charges of misogyny and anti-Americanism.[156] Despite this and not winning any awards at Cannes, *Dogville* received some very positive reviews from critics internationally. For David Thomson, Kidman's 'adventurous instinct has allowed *Dogville* to be made (and to become an international event), so no one really has made such a decisive gesture since Ingrid Bergman did

in 1946 when she gave up a Selznick contract…
to go to Italy to make a film with Roberto
Rossellini, because she believed in his startling
neorealist ways.'[157] The *Village Voice* highlighted
the passion and the originality of 'this austere
allegory of failed Christian charity', calling
the film 'Trier's strongest movie – a masterpiece,
in fact, [in which Kidman] delivers another
remarkable performance.'[158] *Télérama* was full
of praise for Kidman, finding her 'prosaic
and abstract, tender and statuesque, always
captivating, rediscovering incidentally the opacity
of Deneuve in Buñuel's films. She even makes us
forget (was that not the intention?) the formal
experience of the film and allows everyone,
including the viewer, to stay the risky course of
three hours of stylized turpitude.'[159] *Le Point* was
equally enthusiastic: 'Kidman, via a single look,
an attitude, a hint of a gesture, manages to express
the quintessence of her character.'[160] Conversely,
Roger Ebert found that 'Lars von Trier exhibits
the imagination of an artist and the pedantry of a
crank in *Dogville*', but paid tribute to the artist's
'rather brave performance'.[161]

Facing the press, Kidman announced that
she planned to resume her character of Grace
Margaret Mulligan, again under the direction
of von Trier. But the film, *Manderlay* (2005),
was finally shot without her, because of a clash
of schedules or, perhaps, one between the director
and the actress. Kidman, in fact, followed up
with two comedies, *The Stepford Wives* (Frank
Oz, 2004) and *Bewitched* (Nora Ephron, 2005),
nicely sweetened but pertinent satires on the
objectification of American women. Four other
interesting and noteworthy films make up this
post-*Dogville* period: *Birth* (Jonathan Glazer,
2004), *The Interpreter* (Sydney Pollack, 2005),
*Fur: An Imaginary Portrait of Diane Arbus*
(Steven Shainberg, 2006) and *Australia*
(Baz Luhrmann, 2008). However, with *Rabbit
Hole* (2010), which focused on a particularly
sensitive topic and was her first film as a producer,
Kidman chose once more the option of intensity
and suffering.

Opposite: Grace's fur-collared
coat gives her the air
of a Hollywood star turning up
among common folk.
Kidman, an expert at
portraying duplicity, is plunged
into a world without walls,
where people are stereotyped.

# Becca Corbett

*Rabbit Hole* (2010)
**John Cameron Mitchell**

'Becca bonds with the teenager who has run over her son and gradually finds peace. I was brought up in this stoicism. I come from a family where you had to move forward. There was no question of wallowing in sorrow or revealing your emotions or fears.'[162]
Nicole Kidman, 2011

After several films that excited neither audiences nor critics – including *The Invasion* by Oliver Hirschbiegel in 2007 and *Nine* by Rob Marshall in 2009 – *Rabbit Hole* arrived at a time when Kidman was continuing to revive both her personal life (she had married Keith Urban in 2006 and gave birth to a baby girl in 2008) and her career. In 2010, she became a producer, creating Blossom Films, for whom *Rabbit Hole* was the first project. The media delighted in reporting the story: 'Lately, Nicole Kidman has been keeping a low profile. After a series of failures, including notably *Australia*, and less extravagant advertising contracts (she has changed Chanel for Schweppes), the star had moreover arrived at the top of Forbes 2008 list of Hollywood's least profitable stars. Weary of film sets, Nicole Kidman had retired to her farm bought for $2.5 million, in Tennessee, [where] for a year she was living quietly as a mother with her husband, country music star Keith Urban, and their little daughter Sunday Rose. At least, this is what we thought, until late this summer passers-by spotted her in New York on a shoot in the Queens neighbourhood.'[163]

Suppressing Emotion

Making *Rabbit Hole*, which was shot in less than a month, was an intense experience due to its particularly sensitive subject: a few months after Becca Corbett (Nicole Kidman) and her husband Howie (Aaron Eckhart) lost their four-year-old son, run over by a car in front of their house, Becca tries to make contact with Jason (Miles Teller), the teenager responsible for the death of her child. The director, John Cameron Mitchell, who as a fourteen-year-old had experienced the death of his four-year-old brother, described the emotional atmosphere during the making of the film: 'Nicole is in a sort of trance on set. I felt as though I too was performing behind the camera,

and feeling all the emotions she was experiencing. For the scene where she finally breaks down and allows the tears to flow, we did only one take. I was deeply moved, I felt very close to her and, afterwards, I stayed in the car with her, holding her hand.'[164] Similarly, the scene of the argument between Becca and Howie left its mark on the director: 'That scene was terrible to shoot. I felt as though I were a marriage counsellor, because Nicole and Aaron were very aggressive with each other, even between takes. They were so immersed in their characters.'[165]

Eckhart, who is neither a father nor married, struggled to find his character and admitted to having had disagreements with his co-star during filming: 'She was irritated with me and I was irritated with her but that's the way movie-making is. For one day, are we not allowed? For half a day even? […] It's so surprising to me when people are surprised that movie-making is sometimes tense and uncomfortable, because inherently it's going to be.'[166] The twenty-three-old Teller, making his feature-film début, spoke about the development of his relationship with the film's star, which mirrored the growing bond between Jason and Becca: 'For the first scene we did, there wasn't much talking between takes. By the second park scene, there was a little more getting to know Nicole a little bit, and by the third scene even more so. So really it was just an organic evolution of conversation, and getting to know someone. But by the end of it at the wrap party, we were bowling together and laughing and talking about all these things. She's absolutely different.'[167] During the takes, Kidman made it a point of honour to control her emotions so as not to overdo it on screen and to remain as poised as possible. 'I needed to be self-controlled, because it's a very difficult subject', she explained. 'To have a director who manipulated that emotion would not have been good.'[168] Determined to find restraint and authenticity, she paid attention to every aspect of her role, including the clothes worn by her character: 'In a film like this, you have to dress people so that there is no attention on a wardrobe, where all just becomes something that doesn't draw the eye. That's the hardest thing. [The costume designer Ann Roth] said to me: "You're five foot ten and we've got to make you look suburban."'[169] So Becca wears loose clothes

Becca, an inconsolable mother, will try to make contact with the teenager responsible for the death of her child.

With her shoulders constantly knotted up, Becca goes through the motions of being a housewife. Surrounded by her son's things, she throws them out on a whim and stands still, dumbfounded.

Opposite: While attending a support group session for bereaved parents with her husband, Howie (Aaron Eckhart), Becca pouts, rolls her eyes, sighs and finally interrupts a couple who declare that they accept the death of their child because they see it as God's will.

Following pages: Incapable of grieving for her son, Becca shuns intimacy with her husband.

in pastel colours that seem to camouflage her. Her minimal make-up and her hair parted clumsily in the middle put the finishing touches to a deliberately neglected look. The actress explained the principles that guide the film: 'I think [the audience] can expect to be moved, to laugh, to glimpse a period of time in a couple's life they love and know. It's a little voyeuristic. But because of that we realize we're not alone and hopefully it takes away some fear of the worst things that could happen to us. And we can survive.'[170]

Surviving the Death of a Child

Kidman surprises us with the new transformation that she reveals in *Rabbit Hole*, reinventing a whole palette of gestures and attitudes to portray her character. From the very beginning we sense an atmosphere of unease, Becca changing from one mood to another too quickly – from fear, to joy, to irritation, to sadness. Something is wrong in this house and with this couple: she is tearful while her husband watches a video, alone in the dark. She dares not interfere and disappears. But growing weary of acting as if nothing has happened, while attending a support group session for bereaved parents, she pouts, raises her eyes to the ceiling, sighs and finally interrupts a couple who declare that they accept the death of their child because they see it as God's will. She

is exasperated, but conscious of the disturbance she has caused by cutting short the meeting. Kidman plays out this act of defiance while smiling, which we do not expect, even though the way in which she made light, a little earlier, of the news of her sister's pregnancy – with a forced smile and tense movements – already hinted at a certain underlying agitation. The actress conveys to us that Becca is actually containing a huge amount of inner rage. She seems alienated by her daily life: going through the motions of being a housewife, waiting patiently for her washing machine to finish its cycle, while holding her laundry basket. With her shoulders constantly knotted up (as her husband tells her), Becca seems dazed, as though shaken by the shock. Surrounded by her son's things, she decides to get rid of them, which Howie does not understand because he is not there day in day out, in this house haunted by the death of their child. Kidman again plays a preoccupied woman, doomed to survive despite death, continuing her reflection on grief a few years after playing in *Birth* (Jonathan Glazer, 2004).

Becca's anger gradually intensifies. She becomes more and more irritated by her family's behaviour and conversation. Out bowling, she cannot stand to hear her mother comparing the death of her drug-addict son with that of her grandson, mown down by a car when he was still a child, which seems to trivialize his death.

She raises her voice, and we sense that she is close to tears, but she manages to pull herself together. A particularly realistic domestic scene finishes in a row between the Corbetts. At the end of the argument, Becca raises her tense hands, her bent fingers in front of her, as though she wants to cling onto something or grab hold of a ghost. She needs, at this moment, to express, to extract even, her unfathomable grief. Words are not enough, it is her body alone that speaks and screams.

'Becca's actions can be cruel', commented *CNN* reviewer Tom Charity. 'She's cold with Howie, can't disguise her contempt for group therapy (she quits before they throw her out), and she mortifies her husband when she gives away their son's wardrobe without a word of warning. She keeps her emotions locked tight. But unlike Howie, we can see what it costs her, having those clothes in the house. When she starts stalking the teenager who killed her boy, we have no way of knowing which way she'll jump – it's an irrational urge that Kidman makes utterly and immediately human.'[171] After the young man's confession to his involvement in the death of her son, Becca, overwhelmed with emotion, can no longer speak. She emits just a barely audible 'OK'. Their relationship is set in a parallel world: sitting on a bench, they talk to each other in a space–time bubble, far from their respective households. We might even believe, for a while, that this is a fantasy relationship imagined by Becca, particularly as she tells no one about it. Shrouded in long dresses, she stumbles through the grieving process as best she can. Liberating discussions with Howie and Jason are not enough. Kidman makes this clear when, in a supermarket, Becca suddenly slaps a woman she doesn't know, who is refusing to buy candies for her child. A few scenes later, in her car, Becca breaks down in tears, watching Jason carrying on his life as though nothing has happened. This highlights for us the contradictions within each of the couple's reactions: she wants to erase all traces of her son (including drawings, clothes and toys) yet remains stuck in the past, while Howie, who is eager to move forward, is loathe to get rid of his son's things.

While browsing through a comic book that Jason has written, Becca notices the story of Orpheus and Eurydice. According to reviewer Léo Soesanto, 'Kidman escapes into a comic book entitled *Rabbit Hole*, a digression on parallel universes drawn by the teenager responsible for the death of her son – the author of the graphic novel is in fact Dash Shaw, an excellent American cartoonist whose garish drawings, both tender and disturbed, break with the film's torpor. Sitting on a bench, Kidman is able to daydream about a world where she would be happier. And we touch on an everyday moment of strangeness that recalls the top current science-fiction series, *Fringe*. Her relationship with the teenager is the most troubling aspect of the film because Nicole Kidman marvellously assembles contradictory feelings (harassment? desire? forgiveness?), culminating in a beautiful scene where she sees him on the day of his prom.'[172]

Becca does not want to believe in God but she is interested in mythology and parallel universes, and gazes at the sky. Eventually she copes with the loss of her child by being sociable, inviting people over to the house and showing an interest in others. Bereavement is made possible, the actress conveys to us, only through pretence and the imagination. The film's final image shows Kidman breathing deeply. Is this a sign of ultimate suffocation, of tears about to brim over, or rather of a rebirth? 'We know that, from *To Die For* to *Birth*, Kidman's movies successfully draw their unease from the sum of Kidman + teenager or child, quick to break down families and preconceptions', Soesanto notes. 'Here, the actress's features are rather frozen (it's called maturity). And in a final dialogue on the future of their marriage, which echoes *Eyes Wide Shut*, she can leave the last word to her husband. The confident "Fuck" of Kubrick's film is replaced by "And then what?", which is seemingly more comfortable but still on the brink of the unknown.'[173]

Engaging as an Actress and a Woman

For Mitchell, Kidman 'was as naked as she can be, especially considering how the character is put together. But shooting on the Red [movie camera] with soft lenses – we were worried about a hard video look – was a good match. We didn't glam her up; she's a beautiful woman anyway. But for the first time, she feels like she's her age. She wasn't afraid of the shots where she just doesn't look good – weeping, this and that. She went all the way.'[174] The role was a sort of emotional summit for Kidman, who admitted that 'The most terrifying thing I've ever done is to play a mother who loses her child.'[175] In good faith, the actress wanted to explore this dark area (which she had only touched on in *Dead Calm*): 'I tend to go creatively to places that terrify me … [This story] is almost like a minefield.'[176] All this suffering portrayed on screen, added to her list of already particularly intense and sometimes morbid previous roles, branded her as an artist of loss. Speaking of Greta Garbo, the writer and film critic Béla Balázs claimed that her beauty was 'a beauty of suffering; she suffers life and all the surrounding world. And this sadness, this sorrow is a very definite one: the sadness of loneliness, of an estrangement which feels no common tie with other human beings.'[177] Kidman's work is in this same vein, although she develops it within the context of everyday contemporary life and ordinary people.

Opposite: This mother's psychological journey will take her through different stages of grief. From left to right, top to bottom: She inadvertently comes across Jason (Miles Teller), the teenager who ran over her son; sorts through her son's things with her mother (Dianne Wiest); gets misunderstood while out bowling; decides to arrange to meet Jason, who is troubled by guilt; loses her temper with a mother in a store; and then falls apart in the car with her sister Izzy, who is expecting a baby herself.

Following pages: Jason brings the comic book he has written to show Becca. Entitled *Rabbit Hole*, it is about parallel universes and the realm of the possible.

Kidman is mother to several children: firstly, Isabella (born in 1992) and Connor (born in 1995), whom she adopted with her ex-husband, Tom Cruise. After marrying Keith Urban in 2006 and several miscarriages, she gave birth to Sunday Rose in 2008, and used a surrogate mother for their second daughter, Faith Margaret in 2010. For the past several years, she has also given her unconditional support to child protection, notably through her work as an ambassador for UNICEF and her donations to Sydney Children's Hospital Foundation and the Dylan Hartung Fund.

Yet, on screen she has often played childless women and has sometimes even taken on roles in films that depict violence toward children: she loses her son in a car crash in *Dead Calm*; in *Rabbit Hole* she cannot stand other people's children; in *To Die For* she kills her husband so as not to have any; in *The Others* she kills her own offspring; in *Dogville* she has children killed in front of their mother; in *Birth* (Jonathan Glazer, 2004) she takes a bath with a young boy and, in another scene, kisses him on the lips; in *The Golden Compass* (Chris Weitz, 2007) she hunts down children and holds them prisoner to remove all traces of personality from them; and in *Stoker* (Park Chan-wook, 2013) she plays an unstable mother.

However, in most of her films, Kidman plays women who end up being neutralized or overwhelmed by children and their ghosts. This is perhaps the best evidence that the actress uses film not only as a place to explore a theme dear to her, but also as a sort of laboratory to study boundaries, the unknown and the invisible. Childhood and magic are indeed very closely linked in her career, whether as Alice in *Eyes Wide Shut*, a character associated with *The Nutcracker* and with the world of toys, or through her relationship with Nullah, the aboriginal boy introduced to *The Wizard of Oz* and to the magic of his ancestors, that her character adopts in *Australia* (Baz Luhrmann, 2008).

Unlike other actresses working in Hollywood, Kidman is not just another girl-woman – she is too tall and mature for that – but an artist who tirelessly explores the inexpressible nature of childhood, this world of double, parallel identities, which is almost a signature theme of her work.

Opposite: Nicole Kidman
and Mia Wasikowska in *Stoker*
(2013) by Park Chan-wook.

Above: Becca wears
loose clothes that seem to
camouflage her. Her minimal
make-up and her hair parted
clumsily in the middle
put the finishing touches to
a deliberately neglected look.

Following pages: With
the film's director, John
Cameron Mitchell. Mitchell
drew inspiration from
his own life in writing
the screenplay for this film.

This might reflect a general shift in focus for female film stars, which ran parallel with changes in status for women in society as a whole. Edgar Morin, writing in 1972, observed that, over the course of several decades, star-goddesses had been shaking off their divine quality: 'Before 1930 a star was not allowed to become pregnant. After 1930 she could become a mother, and an exemplary one at that. So stars began to participate in the everyday life of mortals. No longer were they inaccessible stars, instead they become mediators between heaven and earth. Great girls, sensational women, they attracted hero worship that was about admiration rather than veneration.'[178] Yet, what motivates Kidman is leading her life as a woman and an artist with a moral commitment, living up to all that it means to be human. She admits that she is interested, above all, in human nature, 'including in its darkest aspects… I try to understand the meaning of life, and I love directors who are as much philosophers as they are filmmakers. Unfortunately, most films released today pander to our tendency to channel hop. I want to fight against that. Or perhaps I'm just old-fashioned.'[179]

A Return to Favour with Critics

At the time the film was released, Florence Colombani wrote in *Le Point*, 'As Christian Bale very correctly stated at the Golden Globes,

"There are silent performances and others that explode in your face."… Well, in *Rabbit Hole*, a beautiful classic film, Nicole Kidman is on the side of silence, of inwardness. She reminds us what a great actress has to offer when she decides to take her career seriously again.'[180] Louise Guichard of *Télérama* also hailed her committed comeback: 'Nicole Kidman, who co-produced the film, takes possession of it passionately but soberly, and exudes a subtle unease, between exasperation and held-back tears… She is reaching a more discreet phase of her career: bereavement suits her, if we can put it that way. But her character is not exempt from the transgressive dimension of her great roles of the 2000s.' Guichard concluded, 'With this persistent image of the woman and the husband avoiding really looking at each other yet living side by side, the bereavement film becomes an elegiac reflection on the couple.'[181] For *Rolling Stone*, 'Nicole Kidman is just astonishing in *Rabbit Hole* — subtle, fierce, brutally funny, tender when you least expect it …'[182] Impressed, Roger Ebert believed that 'Celebrity has clouded her image; if she were less glamorous, she would be more praised. Age will only be an asset to her.'[183] Meanwhile, Tom Charity found Kidman 'an intriguing case, a star who can seem trapped beneath her brittle porcelain beauty, but who has also ventured further and wider than most, taking on risky, uncommercial projects like *Dogville*,

*Birth* and the Diane Arbus movie, *Fur*... This time, at least, she can be sure of engaging our sympathies, even if the material is too depressing to bring in large crowds.'[184]

Kidman's performance also received several nominations, notably at the Oscars and the Golden Globes, and won her much esteem from her peers, including Marion Cotillard, who said, in *Variety*, 'Nicole created her character's journey like a meditation. When Becca doesn't protect herself and instead jumps into her pain, not fighting against it but surrendering to it, she takes us with her toward light. I felt what she felt. I cried with her. I understood every fragment of her inner disaster and the way she survived. Nicole is at the same time a rough and a cut diamond. She has a very simple and direct way to enter your heart. She shares her emotion in the most generous way. She is simply one of the world's best actresses.'[185]

Ultimately, however, this low-budget film did not find its audience, but this did not trouble Kidman unduly: 'It's complicated because you're told all the time that you need to remain "bankable". It's like walking through a minefield! All that I want, myself, is to act, but most of the films that interest me will never be made because they're too strange... I would like to have made some great works. I don't think I have yet given a great performance, unlike Isabelle Huppert, for example. There's an exemplary career, spent portraying complicated female characters.'[186]

There was absolutely no reason for Kidman to be ashamed of her roles and her filmography, particularly as, with the role of the adventurer Gertrude Bell in *Queen of the Desert* (2015), she would add Werner Herzog to her list of great directors. In the meantime, she could be especially proud of her interpretation of the legendary actress Grace Kelly, who might be seen as a mirror portrait of her own international status and profession.

The film leaves the future of this couple unresolved; as Howie says, summarizing their uncertainty in one of the last lines of the film, 'And then what?'

Opposite: For the first time in a while, Kidman looks her age. The role of Becca was a sort of emotional summit for the actress.

# Grace Kelly

*Grace of Monaco* (2014)
Olivier Dahan

'Like her, I know what it is to live in a gilded cage and to try to please everyone to the point that you forget yourself.'[187]
Nicole Kidman, 2014

Approaching fifty, Kidman was more beautiful than ever but knew that she would soon be entering the second half of her career. There were not many years left before certain roles would be closed to her. Playing a race against time with the media and the film industry, both so ruthless with regard to the physical decline of stars, she chose to accept the role of Grace Kelly, who, in the screenplay is thirty-three years old, while she herself was forty-six at the time the film was made. It is difficult not to see *Grace of Monaco* as one of her most personal films, given her intimate knowledge of the hidden face of a so-called fairytale life. 'I had seen all Grace Kelly's films a long time before Olivier Dahan hired me for the role', Kidman admitted. 'She was a very great actress who had won an Oscar before meeting Prince Rainier and giving it all up for him. But acting was her passion. When Hitchcock, who had directed her in three films [*Dial M for Murder* and *Rear Window* in 1954, and *To Catch a Thief* in 1955], wanted to work with her again in 1962, she couldn't refuse him. But her obligations as a wife and princess prevented her from accepting. I understand Grace all the more because I myself was married to a great film celebrity.... That's perhaps the real reason that I wanted to make this film.'[188]

At one point younger actresses (including Charlize Theron, Reese Witherspoon, Gwyneth Paltrow and Amy Adams) were considered for the role, but Kidman's international reputation, experience and expressive power prevailed. 'Nicole is really interesting as an actress', said her on-screen partner, Tim Roth (Prince Rainier). 'On the set, she's very refined, very funny, slightly naive at times. It's just not her; she maintains the character, she's motoring the character most of the day.'[189] Drawing on her previous experience in portraying real-life women, Kidman allowed herself some liberties with the facts, pursuing authenticity rather than strictly adhering to hard facts relating to character, place or time. 'We had five months to prepare', she explained. 'I was able gently to enter her skin by watching, listening, absorbing [...] I didn't feel trapped by having to mimic her [...] It was more trying to find her essence [...] We were not in Los Angeles in a studio pretending to be in France, we were in France! I think that imbues the whole thing...'[190]

In the same way that she adopts Grace Kelly's clothing and colours without seeking to mimic her, so the director, Olivier Dahan, and his cinematographer, Eric Gautier, shot the film in anamorphic format (with an aspect ratio of 2.35:1) less in order to copy the widescreen visual style of the 1960s than to explore the psychology of characters who appear small within the frame, like prisoners of their environment. *Grace of Monaco* portrays a woman who is watched by the whole world and yet who is desperately lonely. An American *émigrée* in Monaco, she does not belong to this fairytale land (like the Australian actress when she arrived in Hollywood in the early 1990s) and needs to find her role, in the literal sense of the word: is she the wife of a prince, a loving mother, an actress, or even all those things at the same time? Who, then, is her character? Suffice to say, it was a tailor-made part for an actress as versatile as Kidman.

## Grace and Nicole in Wonderland

The film opens with a quotation from Grace Kelly: 'The idea of my life as a fairytale is itself a fairytale'. But this opening is soon understood to be a false lead, a *trompe-l'œil*. The beautiful Côte d'Azur road that we see turns out to be, in a zoom out, an image projected on a screen, a special effect in front of which a film crew and a white silhouette (Kidman), who has not yet said her name, are at work. Behind the image then, behind the fairytale, a well-oiled machine of the world of showbiz and pretence is at work. The star of the film being shot in front of our very eyes, in this film studio, has not yet shown us her face. She is distant, like an inaccessible goddess. Seen from behind, she gets out of a car and crosses the set. This is Grace Kelly's last film, *High Society* by Charles Walters, which was shot in the same year she got married. The words 'Los Angeles 1956' appear on the screen and, in that moment, this figure seems to single-handedly embody

Drawing on her previous experience in portraying real-life women, Kidman, in *Grace of Monaco*, pursues authenticity rather than strict adherence to hard facts.

a particular time and the glamour of an era: courteous gestures, bright colours, flowing fabrics, floral elegance and so on. Yet, this whole fairytale world is clearly only make-believe, for when the camera, in a long sequence shot, finally reveals the face of the mysterious Hollywood woman in her dressing room, it is in a mirror that we see the star Grace Kelly reflected. She is partially unmasked because we already understand that she is only an image. In the mirror, framed as in a fashion magazine, her expression is somewhat quizzical as she glances sideways. She seems happy, but the silent pause is a question mark, a blank page that is troubled, troubling, unresolved. Her face, which is not completely smooth, not perfect, is a screen that reveals an underlying worry, an intensity that we will need to figure out.

The inaugural complexity of *Grace of Monaco*, like the maze in *Alice's Adventures in Wonderland*, invites us to pass through to the other side of the mirror in a long movement that gathers up spaces and that Kidman's acting seems to reflect: fluid, ample, passing from one room to another, one place to another, often in the movement of walking or a gesture. Like Alice, Grace is both too big and too small for this idyllic world: miniature in the giant corridors of the Palace of Monaco (like Grace Stewart wandering in those of the manor house in *The Others*); too tall for a prince who is shorter than her and is associated more with darkness than light, as is reflected in the many scenes in the palace's gloomy corridors and staircases. In this world of high contrasts, the Monaco of 1961, it is almost as though we were rediscovering the world of Hollywood studios (vast, high-ceilinged empty rooms, like those of film sets). And, indeed, Grace's first appearance as a princess is similar to that in the film's opening sequence: we see her first from behind, then again, playing a role, that of Grace of Monaco, a title, a role, a brand, a job.

---

Performing Two Roles

Kidman manages, here, to constantly play with the dividing line between fiction and reality. She is Grace, princess and actress. The first time we discover her in her role as princess, she accidentally drops a certificate that she was awarding to some children. Her visitor of the day, Alfred Hitchcock (Roger Ashton-Griffiths), watches the scene from behind her and, amused, says to her: 'This is the part where I say, "Cut!"' Grace, who has turned round, seems to be in disguise, hidden behind her glasses, a double-strand pearl necklace around her neck and a delicate scarf tucked inside the collar of her blouse. Several testing years at court have passed and she has adopted a serious, solemn, straight-backed attitude. In private, she assures her

favourite director, 'Hitch, I'm fine', while looking around at her gilded cage – a moment in which her expression makes us aware that she is effectively imprisoned. Her gaze turns in on itself and she withdraws to an inner world. Kidman's ambiguous, fixed smile, which hints at a concealed sorrow whose secret she holds, completes the feeling we have of a suffocating space. Hitchcock encourages her: 'You're still an artist, Gracie, don't forget it.' Grace is thus torn between two unreal lands: Hollywood and Monaco. Where, then, is her reality?

This permanent no-man's-land where she has to evolve, hesitantly learning new steps, is reflected at a reception where she takes part in a political discussion between Prince Rainier and representatives of the French State. She jumps in with both feet, sitting on the arm of the settee, ignoring the protocol that forbids it. With no respect, either, for the codes and behaviour imposed on women of the court – princess though she is – she freely expresses her opinions and finds herself between two worlds: the United States, to which she belongs by birth, and Europe, which she is supposed to embrace and join through her marriage. She is literally caught between two cultures, the Old World of the 1950s, which does not accept the participation of women in political debate, and Modern America, symbolized by Grace's father, who encouraged her to be determined (here we are verging on self-portraiture as Kidman's father taught her to be politically active at a very young age). Surrounded by powerful men, ensconced in their armchairs, Grace, who is looking down on them, seems to be teaching them a lesson, with aloofness, irony, candour and nonchalance. This scene of diplomatic embarrassment leads to a row between the royal couple. A dispute, shown through mirrors placed all around their bedroom, where Grace appears visually divided, quartered, splintered, and where her husband orders her not to express herself. She no longer understands anything about her role: she had thought he loved her for her frankness. Played against a background of fireworks crackling above the Rock of Monaco, this domestic scene contradicts the world of glitz and widens the gulf between the inside and the outside, between what she must and must not say, be and not be.

As Father Tucker (Frank Langella), Grace's confidant, explains to her, life is not a fairytale or a dream, and love is not a beautiful wedding movie. Here, she is no longer a solemn, role-playing figure, but a serious, tear-stained face, seen in close-up, trapped by her environment. Scrutinized by the cameras, brought face-to-face with herself, she examines her situation, searches her heart and defines her place in the world. Like the cursed albatross struggling to take flight, or like a desperate person trying to mourn (a Kidman trademark *par excellence*), Grace

Opposite: The star of the film being shot in front of our very eyes in the first minutes of *Grace of Monaco* has not yet shown us her face. When the camera, in a long sequence shot, finally reveals the face of the mysterious Hollywood woman, it is in a mirror that we see the star Grace Kelly reflected. Her face, which is not completely smooth, not perfect, is a screen that reveals an underlying worry, an intensity that we will need to figure out.

Following pages: Alfred Hitchcock (Roger Ashton-Griffiths), the princess's favourite director, tries to persuade her to return to acting.

Following her success playing Virginia Woolf in *The Hours*, Kidman has specialized in portraying women who have really lived, including Martha Gellhorn (*Hemingway & Gellhorn* by Philip Kaufman, 2012), Patti Lomax (*The Railway Man* by Jonathan Teplitzky, 2013), Grace Kelly (*Grace of Monaco* by Olivier Dahan, 2014) and Gertrude Bell (*Queen of the Desert* by Werner Herzog, 2015). Through these portraits, the actress lets us see this 'quiet determination… that changes the world'.[j] For each role she weighs up the many potential snares of the risks she is taking – imitation, hamming, artificiality, public expectation – and succeeds in bringing emotion and respect to each character. Nevertheless, for Kidman, it is less about being involved in a biopic than in depicting a particular time in a life, offering a personal interpretation, or even inventing, as in *Fur: An Imaginary Portrait of Diane Arbus* (Steven Shainberg, 2006), where she gives free rein to her audacity, particularly in the sex scenes with a stranger who is completely covered in hair (Robert Downey Jr). The film is disturbing and was poorly received by the press. Kidman was even accused of looking nothing like Diane Arbus,[k] despite the fact that this is precisely one of the unsettling intentions of the film and a denial of logic befitting a play by Peter Brook. Even though some have recognized 'the subtle unease that Kidman as always exudes',[l] others wonder about the reasons that have led her to portray so many exceptional women on screen. 'Being sublime comes at a price: moviegoers constantly have to remind themselves that her mind also verges on perfection. Is that why she persists in playing brilliant and tormented women?'[m] We won't venture here into the star's pride, disproportionate or otherwise. More than interpretations, Kidman-style biopics have, most importantly, a perturbing quality, between rewriting and self-portrait, tenderness and tension that is a clever art of inconsistency, parallels, division and depth.

Opposite: Nicole Kidman in *Fur: An Imaginary Portrait of Diane Arbus* (2006) by Steven Shainberg.

Above: Grace in a rare moment of introspection with her confidant on the Rock, Father Tucker (Frank Langella).

Following pages: In the eyes of Prince Rainier (Tim Roth), the princess should conform to protocol and abstain from freely expressing her opinions in public.

announces, 'I don't know how I'm going to keep living with him. I don't know how I'm going to spend the rest of my life in this place where I can't be me', because, she says, her husband is in love with an image of her. Her friend replies, 'And who is that? Grace Kelly, movie star? You invented her. You learned to sit and a kind of walk, and you perfected a certain kind of accent, and you did it beautifully. But now you're just a housewife with two bratty kids, watching a rerun of your wedding day. Is that why you came here Grace? You came here to play the greatest role of your life: Her Serene Highness, Princess Grace of Monaco, Duchess of Valentinois, and one hundred and thirty-seven more titles that come with it.'

## Being Grace and Nicole, a True Invention

Kidman's character gradually comes to understand her place in the world: she has to be Grace of Monaco, a homemade creation that she must fashion herself, within the limits of the tiny margin of freedom that has been tacitly conceded to her in this patriarchal, hierarchical and highly codified system. Ironically, Prince Rainier himself is operating in a restricted territory, which is threatened with shrinking at the same rate as France – with its plans to annex the Principality – is growing. He, too, is condemned to play a role. France wants to colonize Monaco just as Grace is metaphorically taken hostage by Europe. During

a family scene, Prince Rainier criticizes Grace for having short hair because, in his eyes, she is not supposed to be a modern woman but the princess of a kingdom. And to pull her into line permanently, he says, as an insult, 'You were just an actress.' Alone, Grace can't appeal to her own motherland because when she tries to confide in members of her own family, they dare not speak openly to her, the Princess of Monaco. At this moment, Kidman hardly needs to act out Grace's loneliness. Her vacant eyes, trembling voice, almost at a whisper, sagging shoulders, drooping frame and heavy body all reveal the burdensome life of a superstar.

Even when she escapes the Principality to get some air and to gain a sense of perspective, Grace drives her car in the style of Hollywood movies, with a special-effect background and wearing dark glasses. In short, even her anger is a performance. Kidman perfectly captures this state of affairs: her character seems to want to escape from a fantasy but never succeeds in doing so. When she is sitting on the running board of her sports car, wearing her dark glasses and her scarf, she cannot escape, despite herself, the image of the star – this woman who is beautiful, but frozen in her beauty, like a statue. Yet – and herein lies the irony at the heart of both the role and the film – it is actually the cinema, staging and disguise that will save Grace. Finally taking her role as princess seriously, she wants to learn all there is

Opposite: After the scene in which she puts her husband in a position of diplomatic embarrassment, Grace isolates herself in her room. She appears visually divided, splintered, compelled to repress her personality as a free woman. Her face, trapped by her environment, becomes gradually harder until she decides she must fashion herself, within the limits of the tiny margin of freedom that has been tacitly conceded to her in this patriarchal, hierarchical and highly codified system (last image).

Above: The royal couple come together on the issue of the preservation of the principality, which is threatened by the colonial ambitions of the French government.

Following pages: During an incognito stroll around the principality, the charm of the actress–princess emerges and gradually reverses public opinion. This is where she belongs, this is her identity: in fabrication and fidelity, invention and authenticity.

to know about etiquette, customs and protocol, because no one has yet provided her with the script. French lessons, deportment, all aspects are covered. She must also repeat parrot-fashion what she is told and play out different emotions that will serve her well in society: anger, arrogance, confidence, serenity, regret. Grace becomes an actress again, but this time in the service of politics and history. During one symbolic scene, she becomes a true Trojan horse by taking a basket of refreshments to the French police forces that have made Monaco a prison. She arrives with a smile, speaks to them in French and has them eating out of her hand. The charm of the actress–princess emerges and gradually reverses public opinion in favour of the Rock, with the guidance of Hitchcock himself, who whispers encouragingly: 'Don't stand too close to the edge of the frame.' She becomes a living work of art, while remaining resolutely true to herself, her principles and her intrinsic talents. This is where she belongs, this is her identity: in fabrication and fidelity, invention and authenticity.

This power of fiction over reality manifests itself at an international summit: the red carpet at the reception she has organized, like that at Cannes, enables her to dazzle reality and to stifle family and political intrigues. During the ball she seems to perform a magic trick – of which Kidman holds the secret – by bewitching world leaders,

including President de Gaulle, with her radiance, her ineffable aura. She even goes so far as to kiss her sister-in-law, Princess Antoinette, who she annihilates with a steely gaze, just after having banished her coldly in private, like a Hitchcockian actress. Thanks to her lessons in deportment, Grace inhabits her role and the final speech she makes is a good example. She has totally mastered her role as a princess, and the final image of *Grace of Monaco* remains, in this respect, one of the most representative of all Kidman's work: Grace–Nicole is sitting beneath the lights of a film set, looking at the camera. At this moment it is absolutely impossible to be certain of the nature of the person who meets our awe-struck gaze. A princess? An actress? Nicole Kidman? Grace Kelly? Perhaps this is the pinnacle of the actor's art: to be completely themselves while maintaining an illusion – incredulity as well as doubt – to question how far they can go so as to more effectively create a bond, both physically and spiritually, with the viewer. Ultimately, to be a true invention.

A Controversial Exit

Despite the fairly tame and consensual nature of the film's approach, *Grace of Monaco* sparked a controversy when it was presented at the Cannes Filllm Festival. First of all, the princely family of Monaco expressed their displeasure, issuing

a statement that said: 'The princely family does not in any way wish to be associated with this film which reflects no reality and regrets that its history has been misappropriated for purely commercial purposes.'[191] Dahan responded, explaining that his intention was above all a fictional film about the fate of a particular woman: 'I wasn't the one to "glamorize" the Rock. They are very good at doing that themselves… I am neither a journalist nor an historian. I am an artist. I haven't made a biopic. I detest biopics in general. I have made, completely subjectively, the human portrait of a modern woman who wants to reconcile her family, her husband and her career. But who will give up this career to create a new role for herself. And this will be painful for her. This was what I tried to explain to the Grimaldi family when I met them and I had the feeling then that they had listened… Today, they have changed their minds. But I understand their point of view. After all, she was their mother. I don't want to provoke anyone. Just to say that this is cinema.'[192]

The day before the Cannes official screening and press conference, Kidman reiterated this rebuttal: 'Their reaction really surprised me. I've often made radical choices, and some of my films have been harshly criticized, but this is the first time that I have found myself in the middle of such a controversy. I am a mother, I have children, grown-up and young, and I know that things can be complex for them, like when, for example, the problems in my first marriage were dissected in the press. But Grace's children can understand that this film is a mixture of factual and fictional scenes during the year 1962.'[193]

In addition to this widely reported controversy, there was also the artistic conflict between the director and the United States distributor, Harvey Weinstein, who was dissatisfied with the editing of the film, which added to the ordeal in the press and did nothing to ensure a serene reception for the film. Rumours of an American version, reassembled by the distributor, ruffled more feathers, but it was ultimately the director's cut that was screened at Cannes.[194]

Meanwhile, Nicole also suffered the wrath of the international press. *Le Nouvel Obs* was sceptical about the choice of actress: 'How can you credibly portray a Grace Kelly who is not even thirty when you are forty-six and that fact is blindingly obvious? Although her figure and hairstyle are consistent, we remain more dubious about the embalmed and inexpressive face of the Australian actress… Behind the Botox and glitz, *Grace of Monaco* arouses nothing but disappointment and boredom. Such a central figure in cinema and the history of Monaco deserved a much finer tribute than this glossy melodrama, which is as static as the face of its leading actress. Judging by its very cool reception on the Côte d'Azur, this wretched faux-biopic

seems already destined for disgrace.'[195] *Variety* found the film 'as dramatically inert as star Nicole Kidman's frigid cheek muscles'.[196] But among the general mayhem were a few critics who happily greeted Kidman's performance, in particular Eric Kohn, writing for *Indiewire*: 'Both soft and fierce in every scene, Nicole Kidman skillfully embodies the paradox of Kelly's public life.'[197]

In her book on the actress, Pam Cook speaks of Kidman as a brand that adds value as much to the cinema as to the make-up and beauty cream industries,[198] whereas it would be judicious to see above all an artist who is struggling against her time and has done so since her first memorable roles. The star herself does not seem – from the height of her imaginary pedestal – to forget this, thanks to choices that are often rebellious, as she plays cat and mouse with the audience's expectations, paragons and ways to distinguish herself from them. While her age raised many issues, time will probably, ultimately, play in her favour and, more specifically, in favour of her Grace Kelly, a reflection on her own profession and on her private life.

Much water has flowed under the bridge since Kidman's first Australian films – notably *Dead Calm*. Yet Kidman continues to take on bereaved characters, tragically but magnificently hybrid women, prisoners of enclosed spaces. These are characters, with or without a future, that she draws and redraws, like advancing increasingly nearer to the centre of a moving target. Acting, putting herself in danger, in order to be fully herself, seems to be what is at issue here. Twenty-five years after she emerged onto the public scene, Kidman now says, 'The more I mature, the more I draw influence from elements of my life that can serve my roles.'[199] And she adds, 'It took me until I was in my forties to understand the woman I am, what I wanted to convey to my children and the role that I can play in the world… I would like people to talk about me as someone curious, who has a sense of adventure.'[200]

At the end of the film, during the ball that the Rainiers have organized, Grace performs a magic trick – of which Kidman holds the secret – by bewitching world leaders, including President de Gaulle, with her ineffable charm.

# Conclusion

For various reasons, Kidman has not taken on certain roles: she was nearly Catwoman in *Batman Returns* (Tim Burton, 1992, with Michelle Pfeiffer), Annie Reed in *Sleepless in Seattle* (Nora Ephron, 1993, with Meg Ryan), Jenny Curran in *Forrest Gump* (Robert Zemeckis, 1994, with Robin Wright), Meg Altman in *Panic Room* (David Fincher, 2002, with Jodie Foster), Roxie Hart in *Chicago* (Rob Marshall, 2002, with Renée Zellweger), Frannie Avery in *In the Cut* (Jane Campion, 2003, with Meg Ryan, again), Katharine Hepburn in *The Aviator* (Martin Scorsese, 2004, with Cate Blanchett), Grace Mulligan in *Manderlay* (Lars von Trier, 2005, with Bryce Dallas Howard), Mrs Smith in *Mr. & Mrs. Smith* (Doug Liman, 2005, with Angelina Jolie) and Hanna Schmitz in *The Reader* (Stephen Daldry, 2008, with Kate Winslet). One of her most intriguing aborted projects is *The Lady From Shanghai*, which she should have shot in 2007, directed by Wong Kar Wai. Her filmography, however, is so full of great directors and significant works that it would be churlish to dwell on these missed opportunities.

Although a certain form of academicism is always dangerous for such a well-established, iconic actress, Kidman is, fortunately, likely to remain true to her life and career principles of risk-taking and exploration. 'What I want is to be stimulated. Shaken up. It's in my nature to push the boundaries. The more people try to restrict me, the more I want to rebel.'[201]

Insatiable and indispensable, she is still at the top, after numerous dramas and returns to grace – despite the passing years, which is still a difficult issue for many leading actresses. These living icons, who have spent their lives in the spotlight, find it harder to secure roles as they age. This may seem cruel, but it's the harsh reality of the film industry. Those who have survived the decades and continued to pursue a career as fulfilling and remarkable as that of their earlier years are the exception rather than the rule (Catherine Deneuve is one such example). Audiences and professionals alike are thus demanding the impossible of Kidman – that she remain flawless and exceptional despite the passing of time (her career already spans 30 years), the aggression of the international media and fierce competition.

As Michel Serres writes about statues, 'Lucretia reveals the existence of atoms via the long erosion of idols subjected to the gentle caresses and kisses of worshippers: the stone itself is worn away.'[202] And yet, like a modern-day Scheherazade, the actress is successfully meeting this impossible challenge: she is resisting idolatry, the clock and obscurity. She is a star that continues to shed light on the status of women – a flagship for women, passionate about freedom, whose zeal and energy belie the dumb blonde cliché.

Following pages: Nicole Kidman plays Lady Sarah Ashley in Baz Luhrmann's *Australia* (2008).

**1967**
20 June. Nicole Mary Kidman is born in Honolulu (Hawaii, United States). Her father, Antony, of Australian origin, and her mother, Janelle, of Irish descent, both work in the medical sector. The family settles in Washington, DC, soon after.

**1971**
The Kidmans move to Australia after the birth of their second daughter, Antonia.

**1972**
At the age of five Nicole discovers her vocation as an actress while performing in a Christmas play. She starts taking dancing lessons, then drama classes, in parallel with her schooling.

**1983**
At the age of sixteen she lands her first film role in *Bush Christmas* and quickly follows it with another film, *BMX Bandits*.

**1984**
She interrupts her work to look after her mother, who is suffering from breast cancer, before resuming her studies in dramatic art at the Victorian College of the Arts (Melbourne), then at the Phillip Street Theatre (Sydney), where she meets Naomi Watts, and at the Australian Theatre for Young People (Sydney).

**1987**
First major role in the TV series *Vietnam* (produced by George Miller), for which she receives her first award, from the Australian Film Institute, thanks to which she begins to make a name for herself in Australia.

**1989**
She plays her first major international role, in the thriller *Dead Calm*, opposite Sam Neill. This film opens the doors of Hollywood for her, with the help of her agent, Sam Cohn.

**1990**
Release of *Days of Thunder* by Tony Scott. Her screen partner, Tom Cruise, also becomes her husband, on 24 December. They become the new Hollywood couple.

**1991**
First nomination at the Golden Globes, for *Billy Bathgate*, directed by Robert Benton.

**1993**
The couple adopts their first child, Isabella Jane.

**1994**
Despite several underwhelming films, but thanks to her commitment to children and a significant media presence, Kidman is named Goodwill Ambassador for UNICEF.

**1995**
Her first big leap between Hollywood and independent cinema: the release of the blockbuster *Batman Forever* directed by Joel Schumacher, in which she plays opposite Val Kilmer, and the low-budget film *To Die For* by Gus Van Sant, where she partners Matt Dillon and the young Joaquin Phoenix. Cruise and Kidman adopt their son, Connor Antony. The actress does not wish her children to be raised according to the precepts of Scientology, to which her husband adheres.

**1996**
First Golden Globe, for *To Die For*. She is at last recognized as an actress in her own right, no longer simply as 'the wife of'. Release of *The Portrait of a Lady* by the New Zealand director Jane Campion, who had spotted the actress in the early 1980s.

**1998**
She appears in the play *The Blue Room*, David Hare's adaptation of Arthur Schnitzler's play *Der Reigen*, which enjoys commercial success in New York.

**1999**
After a very long shoot, impeded by rumours concerning Kidman and Cruise's relationship both on and off the set, *Eyes Wide Shut* is released with much media coverage, a few months after the death of its director, Stanley Kubrick.

**2001**
A particularly busy year: the actress plays supporting roles in three very different films (*Birthday Girl*, *The Others* and *Moulin Rouge!*) and, on 8 August, is granted a divorce. *People* magazine ranks her among 'The 25 Most Intriguing People' of the year and *Entertainment Weekly* names her Entertainer of the Year.

**2002**
While the media coverage of her divorce rages, she presents *The Hours*, in which she plays the writer Virginia Woolf, a performance for which she receives an Oscar and a Golden Globe.

**2003**
Release of *Cold Mountain* by Anthony Minghella, with Jude Law; *The Human Stain* by Robert Benton, with Anthony Hopkins; and, particularly noteworthy, *Dogville* by Lars von Trier, in which the actress smashes her Hollywood star image.

**2004**
Release of *Birth* by Jonathan Glazer. Although generally well received by the critics, it is a commercial flop.

**2005**
Release of *Bewitched* by Nora Ephron, for which the actress's fee rose to $17 million. In a completely different vein, *The Interpreter* by Sydney Pollack gives her the opportunity to act opposite Sean Penn.

**2006**
She lends her voice to the animated film *Happy Feet* by George Miller and plays the photographer Diane Arbus in the independent film *Fur* by Steven Shainberg. She is appointed international

spokeswoman for UNIFEM, which campaigns for women's empowerment and gender equality throughout the world. She visits, notably, Kosovo, testifies before Congress, raises millions of dollars in funds and collects as many signatures. She marries Australian country singer Keith Urban on 25 June.

## 2008
Release of the film *Australia* by the Australian director Baz Luhrmann, co-starring Hugh Jackman, a friend of the actress's and a fellow Australian. On 7 July she gives birth for the first time, at the age of forty-one, to a girl, named Sunday Rose.

## 2010
She founds the production company Blossom Films and performs in her first film for the company, *Rabbit Hole*, for which she receives an Oscar nomination. She becomes mother to another girl, Faith Margaret, on 28 December.

## 2012
Presentation at the Cannes Film Festival of *The Paperboy*, directed by Lee Daniels. She also plays Martha Gellhorn, opposite Clive Owen as Ernest Hemingway, in the TV film *Hemingway & Gellhorn* by Philip Kaufman.

## 2013
Member of the 66th Cannes Film Festival jury, chaired by Steven Spielberg.

## 2014
Release of *Grace of Monaco* by Olivier Dahan, in which she plays the actress and princess Grace Kelly. Films *Queen of the Desert* under the direction of Werner Herzog. Death of her father.

## 2015
Stars in several films, including *Strangerlander*,

*The Family Fang* and *Genius*. She returns to the stage, playing the scientist Rosalind Franklin in Anna Ziegler's play *Photograph 51*.

Page 174, clockwise: Nicole Kidman in Ken Cameron's *Bangkok Hilton* (1989), Tony Scott's *Days of Thunder* (1990), Robert Benton's *The Human Stain* (2003) and Joel Schumacher's *Batman Forever* (1996).

Opposite, clockwise: Nicole Kidman in Frank Oz's *The Stepford Wives* (2004), Chris Weitz's *The Golden Compass* (2007), Werner Herzog's *Queen of the Desert* (2015) and Park Chan-wook's *Stoker* (2013).

Page 178, clockwise: Posters for Nora Ephron's *Bewitched* (2005), Sydney Pollack's *The Interpreter* (2005), Oliver Hirschbiegel's *The Invasion* (2007) and Steven Shainberg's *Fur: An Imaginary Portrait of Diane Arbus* (2006).

Page 189: Nicole Kidman in Anthony Minghella's *Cold Mountain* (2003).

**1983**
*Skin Deep* (TV)
*Direction* Mark Joffe and Chris Langman *Screenplay* Anne Lucas *Cinematography* Ray Henman *Production* Stanley Walsh *Cast* Briony Behets (Barbara Kennedy), Paul Dawber (Frank Hudson), Nicole Kidman (Sheena Henderson).

*Bush Christmas*
*Direction* Henri Safran *Screenplay* Ted Roberts *Cinematography* Ross Berryman and Malcolm Richards *Production Design* Darrell Lass *Costumes* Utopia Road *Editing* Ron Williams *Music* Mike Perjanik *Production* Gilda Baracchi and Paul D. Barron *Cast* John Ewart (Bill), John Howard (Sly), Nicole Kidman (Helen).

*BMX Bandits*
*Direction* Brian Trenchard-Smith *Screenplay* Patrick Edgeworth and Russell Hagg *Cinematography* John Seale *Production Design* Ross Major *Costumes* Lesley McLennan *Editing* Alan Lake *Music* Colin Stead and Frank Strangio *Production* Tom Broadbridge, Paul F. Davies and Brian Burgess *Cast* David Argue (Whitey), John Ley (Moustache), Nicole Kidman (Judy).

*Chase Through the Night* (TV)
*Direction* Howard Rubie *Screenplay* Rob George and Josephine Emery (as John Emery), from the novel by Max Fatchen *Cinematography* Ernie Clark *Production Design* Ken James

*Costumes* Fiona Spence *Editing* Bob Cogger *Music* Richard Mills *Production* Jim George and Brendon Lunney *Cast* Ron Blanchard (Mert), Brett Climo (Ray), Nicole Kidman (Petra).

**1984**
*A Country Practice* (TV series)
'Repairing the Damage'
Season 4, episode 44
*Direction* Gary Conway *Screenplay* Forrest Redlich *Production Design* Steve Muir *Music* Mike Perjanik *Cast* Shane Porteous (Dr Terrence Elliot), Joyce Jacobs (Esme Watson), Nicole Kidman (Simone Jenkins).

*Matthew and Son* (TV)
*Direction* Gary Conway *Screenplay* Marcus Cole and Bert Deling *Cinematography* Ellery Ryan *Production* Damien Parer *Cast* Douglas Bennett (Mr Hutchins), Paul Cronin (Matthew Caine), Nicole Kidman (Bridget Elliot).

**1985**
*Winners* (TV series)
'Room to Move' (season 1, episode 1)
*Direction* John Duigan *Screenplay* John Duigan *Cinematography* Michael Edols *Costumes* Sian Pugh *Editing* Frans Vandenburg *Music* William Motznig *Production* Julia Overton and Richard Mason *Cast* Nicole Kidman (Carol Trig), Alyssa-Jane Cook (Angie Spry), Terence Donovan (Peter Trig), Veronica Lang (Alison Trig), Martin Harris (Bruce Spry).

*Five Mile Creek* (TV series)
Season 3, episodes 1–13
*Direction* Kevin James Dobson, Brendan Maher, Gary Conway and Brian Trenchard-Smith *Screenplay* Sarah Crawford, Peter A. Kinloch, Denise Morgan, Tom Hegarty and Keith Thompson, from the novel *The Cherokee Trail* by Louis l'Amour. *Cinematography* Kevan Lind *Production Design* George Liddle *Editing* Stuart Armstrong and Marc van Buuren *Music* Bruce Smeaton *Cast* Louise Caire Clark (Maggie Scott), Rod Mullinar (Jack Taylor), Liz Burch (Kate Wallace), Michael Caton (Paddy Malone), Jay Kerr (Con Madigan), Nicole Kidman (Annie), Di O'Connor (Ethel).

*Wills & Burke*
*Direction* Bob Weis *Screenplay* Philip Dalkin *Cinematography* Nino Gaetano Martinetti *Production Design* Tracy Watt *Costumes* Rose Ching and Karen Merkel *Editing* Edward McQueen-Mason *Music* Paul Grabowsky and Red Symons *Production* Margot McDonald and Bob Weis *Cast* Garry McDonald (Robert O'Hara Burke), Kim Gyngell (William John Wills), Nicole Kidman (Julia Matthews).

*Archer* (TV)
*Direction* Denny Lawrence *Screenplay* Anne Brooksbank *Cinematography* Frank Hammond *Production Design* John Parker and

Herbert Pinter *Costumes* Anna Senior *Editing* Ted Otton *Music* Chris Neal *Production* Moya Iceton *Cast* Brett Climo (Dave Power), Robert Coleby (Etienne de Mestre), Ned Lander (Jack Cutts), Nicole Kidman (Catherine).

**1986**
*Windrider*
*Direction* Vincent Monton *Screenplay* Everett De Roche and Bonnie Harris *Cinematography* Joseph Pickering *Production Design* Phil Peters *Costumes* Noel Howell *Editing* John Scott *Music* Kevin Peek *Production* Paul D. Barron *Cast* Tom Burlinson (Stewart 'P. C.' Simpson), Nicole Kidman (Jade), Jill Perryman (Miss Dodge).

**1987**
*Un'Australiana a Roma* (TV)
*Direction* Sergio Martino *Screenplay* Massimo De Rita, Lorraine De Selle and Luigi Spagnol *Cinematography* Roberto Gerardi *Costumes* Francesco Crivellini *Editing* Eugenio Alabiso *Music* Luciano Michelini *Production* Luciano Martino and Lorraine de Selle *Cast* Massimo Ciavarro, Nicole Kidman (Jill), Lara Wendel, Maurizio Mattioli.

*Vietnam* (mini-series)
*Direction* John Duigan and Chris Noonan *Screenplay* John Duigan, Francine Finnane, Terry Hayes, Chris Noonan and Phillip Noyce *Cinematography* Geoff Burton *Costumes* Kristian

Fredrikson *Editing* Neil Thumpston *Production* Terry Hayes, George Miller and Doug Mitchell *Cast* Nicole Kidman (Megan Goddard), Pauline Chan (Lien), Veronica Lang (Evelyn Goddard), Barry Otto (Douglas Goddard).

### Nightmaster (a.k.a. Watch the Shadows Dance)
*Direction* Mark Joffe *Screenplay* Michael McGennan *Cinematography* Martin McGrath *Production Design* Michael Ralph *Costumes* Helen Hooper *Editing* Lindsay Frazer *Music* David Skinner *Production* Jan Tyrrell and James M. Vernon *Cast* Tom Jennings (Robby Mason), Nicole Kidman (Amy Gabriel), Joanne Samuel (Sonia Spane).

### The Bit Part
*Direction* Brendan Maher *Screenplay* Ian McFadyen, Steve Vizard and Peter Herbert *Cinematography* Ellery Ryan *Production Design* Carole Harvey *Costumes* Ruben Thomas *Editing* Scott McLennan *Music* Paul Grabowsky and Red Symons *Production* John Gauci, Peter Herbert and Steve Vizard *Cast* Chris Haywood (Michael Thornton), Nicole Kidman (Mary McAllister), Katrina Foster (Helen Thornton), John Wood (John Bainbridge).

### Room to Move (TV)
*Direction* John Duigan *Screenplay* John Duigan *Cinematography* Michael Edols *Production Design* Louella Hatfield *Costumes* Sian Pugh *Editing* Frans Vandenburg *Music* William Motzing *Production* Richard Mason and Julia Overton *Cast* Nicole Kidman (Carole Trig), Alyssa-Jane Cook (Angie Spry), Terence Donovan (Peter Trig), Veronica Lang (Alison Trig),

Martin Harris (Bruce Spry), Emma Lyle (Andrea Trig), Helen Pankhurst (Jenny Forenko).

## 1988
### Emerald City
*Direction* Michael Jenkins *Screenplay* David Williamson, from his play *Cinematography* Paul Murphy *Production Design* Owen Williams *Costumes* Anthony Jones *Editing* Neil Thumpston *Music* Chris Neal *Production* Joan Long *Cast* John Hargreaves (Colin Rogers), Nicole Kidman (Helen McCord), Chris Haywood (Mike McCord), Robyn Nevin (Kate Rogers).

## 1989
### Dead Calm
*Direction* Phillip Noyce *Screenplay* Terry Hayes, from the novel by Charles Williams *Cinematography* Dean Semler *Production Design* Graham 'Grace' Walker *Costumes* Norma Moriceau *Editing* Richard Francis-Bruce *Music* Graeme Revell *Production* Terry Hayes, George Miller and Doug Mitchell *Cast* Nicole Kidman (Rae Ingram), Sam Neill (John Ingram), Billy Zane (Hughie Warriner).

### Bangkok Hilton (mini-series)
*Direction* Ken Cameron *Screenplay* Ken Cameron, Terry Hayes and Tony Morphett *Cinematography* Geoff Burton *Production Design* Owen Williams *Costumes* Glenys Jackson *Editing* Marcus d'Arcy, Henry Dangar, Louise Innes and Frans Vandenburg *Production* Terry Hayes, George Miller and Doug Mitchell *Cast* Nicole Kidman (Katrina Stanton), Denholm Elliott (Hal Stanton), Hugo Weaving (Richard Carlisle), Noah Taylor (Billy Engels).

## 1990
### Days of Thunder
*Direction* Tony Scott *Screenplay* Robert Towne

*Cinematography* Ward Russell *Production Design* Thomas Sanders *Costumes* Susan Becker *Editing* Robert C. Jones, Chris Lebenzon, Bert Lovitt, Michael Tronick, Stuart Waks and Billy Weber *Music* Hans Zimmer *Production* Jerry Bruckheimer and Don Simpson *Cast* Tom Cruise (Cole Trickle), Nicole Kidman (Dr Claire Lewicki), Robert Duvall (Harry Hogge), Randy Quaid (Tim Daland), Cary Elwes (Russ Wheeler), John C. Reilly (Buck Bretherton).

## 1991
### Flirting
*Direction* John Duigan *Screenplay* John Duigan *Cinematography* Geoff Burton *Production Design* Roger Ford *Editing* Robert Gibson *Production* Terry Hayes, George Miller and Doug Mitchell *Cast* Noah Taylor (Danny Embling), Thandie Newton (Thandiwe Adjewa), Nicole Kidman (Nicola), Naomi Watts (Janet Odgers).

### Billy Bathgate
*Direction* Robert Benton *Screenplay* Tom Stoppard, from the novel by E. L. Doctorow *Cinematography* Néstor Almendros *Production Design* Patrizia von Brandenstein *Costumes* Joseph G. Aulisi *Editing* Alan Heim, David Ray and Robert M. Reitano *Music* Mark Isham *Production* Robert F. Colesberry and Arlene Donovan *Cast* Dustin Hoffman (Dutch Schultz), Nicole Kidman (Drew Preston), Loren Dean (Billy Bathgate), Bruce Willis (Bo Weinberg), Steven Hill (Otto Berman), Steve Buscemi (Irving).

## 1992
### Far and Away
*Direction* Ron Howard *Screenplay* Bob Dolman *Cinematography* Mikael Salomon *Production Design*

Allan Cameron and Jack T. Collis *Costumes* Joanna Johnston *Editing* Daniel P. Hanley and Mike Hill *Music* John Williams *Production* Brian Grazer and Ron Howard *Cast* Tom Cruise (Joseph Donnelly), Nicole Kidman (Shannon Christie), Thomas Gibson (Stephen Chase), Robert Prosky (Daniel Christie), Barbara Babcock (Nora Christie).

## 1993
### Malice
*Direction* Harold Becker *Screenplay* Aaron Sorkin and Scott Frank *Cinematography* Gordon Willis *Production Design* Philip Harrison *Costumes* Michael Kaplan *Editing* David Bretherton *Music* Jerry Goldsmith *Production* Harold Becker, Charles Mulvehill and Rachel Pfeffer *Cast* Alec Baldwin (Jed), Nicole Kidman (Tracy), Bill Pullman (Andy), Bebe Neuwirth (Dana), George C. Scott (Dr Kessler), Anne Bancroft (Ms Kennsinger).

### My Life
*Direction* Bruce Joel Rubin *Screenplay* Bruce Joel Rubin *Cinematography* Peter James *Production Design* Neil Spisak *Costumes* Judy L. Ruskin *Editing* Richard Chew *Music* John Barry *Production* Hunt Lowry, Bruce Joel Rubin and Jerry Zucker *Cast* Michael Keaton (Bob Jones), Nicole Kidman (Gail Jones), Bradley Whitford (Paul Ivanovich), Queen Latifah (Theresa), Michael Constantine (Bill Ivanovich).

## 1995
### To Die For
*Direction* Gus Van Sant *Screenplay* Buck Henry, from the novel by Joyce Maynard *Cinematography* Eric Alan Edwards *Production Design* Missy Stewart *Costumes* Beatrix Aruna Pasztor *Editing* Curtiss Clayton *Music* Danny Elfman *Production* Laura Ziskin *Cast* Nicole Kidman

(Suzanne Stone Maretto), Matt Dillon (Larry Maretto), Joaquin Phoenix (Jimmy Emmett), Casey Affleck (Russel Hines), Illeana Douglas (Janice Maretto), Alison Folland (Lydia Mertz), Dan Hedaya (Joe Maretto), Wayne Knight (Ed Grant), Kurtwood Smith (Earl Stone).

### Batman Forever
*Direction* Joel Schumacher *Screenplay* Lee Batchler, Janet Scott Batchler and Akiva Goldsman, from characters by Bob Kane *Cinematography* Stephen Goldblatt *Production Design* Barbara Ling *Costumes* Ingrid Ferrin and Bob Ringwood *Editing* Mark Stevens and Dennis Virkler *Music* Elliot Goldenthal *Production* Tim Burton and Peter MacGregor-Scott *Cast* Val Kilmer (Batman/Bruce Wayne), Tommy Lee Jones (Two-Face/Harvey Dent), Jim Carrey (Riddler/Dr Edward Nygma), Nicole Kidman (Dr Chase Meridian), Chris O'Donnell (Robin/Dick Grayson).

## 1996
### The Portrait of a Lady
*Direction* Jane Campion *Screenplay* Laura Jones, from the novel by Henry James *Cinematography* Stuart Dryburgh *Production Design* Janet Patterson *Costumes* Janet Patterson *Editing* Veronika Jenet *Music* Wojciech Kilar *Production* Steve Golin and Monty Montgomery *Cast* Nicole Kidman (Isabel Archer), John Malkovich (Gilbert Osmond), Barbara Hershey (Madame Serena Merle), Mary-Louise Parker (Henrietta Stackpole), Richard E. Grant (Lord Warburton), Christian Bale (Edward Rosier), Viggo Mortensen (Caspar Goodwood).

## 1997
### The Peacemaker
*Direction* Mimi Leder *Screenplay* Michael Schiffer, from an article by Leslie Redlich Cockburn and Andrew Cockburn *Cinematography* Dietrich Lohmann *Production Design* Leslie Dilley *Costumes* Shelley Komarov *Editing* David Rosenbloom *Music* Hans Zimmer *Production* Branko Lustig and Walter Parkes *Cast* George Clooney (Lt. Col. Thomas Devoe), Nicole Kidman (Dr Julia Kelly), Marcel Iures (Dusan Gavrich), Aleksandr Baluev (General Aleksandr Kodoroff).

## 1998
### Practical Magic
*Direction* Griffin Dunne *Screenplay* Adam Brooks, Akiva Goldsman and Robin Swicord, from the novel by Alice Hoffman *Cinematography* Andrew Dunn *Production Design* Robin Standefer *Costumes* Judianna Makovsky *Editing* Elizabeth Kling *Music* Alan Silvestri *Production* Denise di Novi *Cast* Sandra Bullock (Sally Owens), Nicole Kidman (Gillian Owens), Stockard Channing (Aunt Frances), Dianne Wiest (Aunt jet), Goran Visnjic (Jimmy Angelov), Aidan Quinn (Gary Hallet), Evan Rachel Wood (Kylie).

## 1999
### Eyes Wide Shut
*Direction* Stanley Kubrick *Screenplay* Stanley Kubrick and Frederic Raphael, from the novella by Arthur Schnitzler *Production Design* Leslie Tomkins and Roy Walker *Costumes* Marit Allen *Editing* Nigel Galt *Music* Jocelyn Pook *Production* Stanley Kubrick *Cast* Tom Cruise (Dr William Harford), Nicole Kidman (Alice Harford), Sydney Pollack (Victor Ziegler), Marie Richardson (Marion), Rade Serbedzija (Milich), Todd Field (Nick Nightingale).

## 2001
### Moulin Rouge!
*Direction* Baz Luhrmann *Screenplay* Baz Luhrmann and Craig Pearce *Cinematography* Donald McAlpine *Production Design* Catherine Martin *Costumes* Catherine Martin and Angus Strathie *Editing* Jill Bilcock *Music* Craig Armstrong *Production* Fred Baron, Martin Brown and Baz Luhrmann *Cast* Nicole Kidman (Satine), Ewan McGregor (Christian), John Leguizamo (Henri de Toulouse-Lautrec), Jim Broadbent (Harold Zidler), Richard Roxburgh (The Duke).

### The Others
*Direction* Alejandro Amenábar *Screenplay* Alejandro Amenábar *Cinematography* Javier Aguirresarobe *Production Design* Benjamín Fernández *Costumes* Sonia Grande *Editing* Nacho Ruiz Capillas *Music* Alejandro Amenábar *Production* Fernando Bovaira, José Luis Cuerda and Sunmin Park *Cast* Nicole Kidman (Grace Stewart), Fionnula Flanagan (Mrs Bertha Mills), Christopher Eccleston (Charles Stewart), Alakina Mann (Anne Stewart), James Bentley (Nicholas Stewart).

### Birthday Girl
*Direction* Jez Butterworth *Screenplay* Jez Butterworth and Tom Butterworth *Cinematography* Oliver Stapleton *Production Design* Hugo Luczyc-Wyhowski *Costumes* Phoebe De Gaye *Editing* Christopher Tellefsen *Music* Stephen Warbeck *Production* Steve Butterworth and Diana Phillips. With Nicole Kidman (Sophia, alias Nadia), Ben Chaplin (John), Vincent Cassel (Alexei), Mathieu Kassovitz (Yuri).

## 2002
### The Hours
*Direction* Stephen Daldry *Screenplay* David Hare, from the novel by Michael Cunningham *Cinematography* Seamus McGarvey *Production Design* Maria Djurkovic *Costumes* Ann Roth *Editing* Peter Boyle *Music* Philip Glass *Production* Robert Fox and Scott Rudin *Cast* Meryl Streep (Clarissa Vaughan), Julianne Moore (Laura Brown), Nicole Kidman (Virginia Woolf), Ed Harris (Richard Brown), Toni Collette (Kitty), Claire Danes (Julia Vaughan), Jeff Daniels (Louis Waters).

## 2003
### Dogville
*Direction* Lars von Trier *Screenplay* Lars von Trier *Cinematography* Anthony Dod Mantle *Production Design* Peter Grant *Costumes* Manon Rasmussen *Editing* Molly Malene Stensgaard *Production* Vibeke Windeløv *Cast* Nicole Kidman (Grace Margaret Mulligan), Paul Bettany (Tom Edison), Lauren Bacall (Ma Ginger), Stellan Skarsgård (Chuck), Chloë Sevigny (Liz Henson), Ben Gazzara (Jack McKay), James Caan (The Big Man), John Hurt (Narrator).

### The Human Stain
*Direction* Robert Benton *Screenplay* Nicholas Meyer, from the novel by Philip Roth *Cinematography* Jean-Yves Escoffier *Production Design* David Gropman *Costumes* Rita Ryack *Editing* Christopher Tellefsen *Music* Rachel Portman *Production* Gary Lucchesi, Tom Rosenberg and Scott Steindorff *Cast* Anthony Hopkins (Coleman Silk), Nicole Kidman (Faunia Farley), Ed Harris (Lester Farley), Gary Sinise (Nathan Zuckerman), Wentworth Miller (Young Coleman Silk).

### Cold Mountain
*Direction* Anthony Minghella *Screenplay* Anthony Minghella, from the novel by Charles Frazier *Cinematography* John Seale *Production Design* Dante Ferretti *Costumes* Carlo Poggioli and Ann Roth *Editing* Walter Murch

*Music* Gabriel Yared *Production* Albert Berger, William Horberg, Sydney Pollack and Ron Yerxa *Cast* Jude Law (Inman), Nicole Kidman (Ada Monroe), Renée Zellweger (Ruby Thewes), Eileen Atkins (Maddy), Brendan Gleeson (Stobrod Thewes), Philippe Seymour Hoffman (Reverend Veasey), Natalie Portman (Sara).

## 2004
### The Stepford Wives
*Direction* Frank Oz *Screenplay* Paul Rudnick, from the novel by Ira Levin *Cinematography* Rob Hahn *Production Design* Jackson DeGovia *Costumes* Ann Roth *Editing* Jay Rabinowitz *Music* David Arnold *Production* Donald De Line, Gabriel Grunfeld, Scott Rudin and Edgar J. Scherick *Cast* Nicole Kidman (Joanna Eberhart), Matthew Broderick (Walter Kresby), Bette Midler (Bobbie Markowitz), Glenn Close (Claire Wellington), Christopher Walken (Mike Wellington).

### Birth
*Direction* Jonathan Glazer *Screenplay* Jean-Claude Carrière, Milo Addica and Jonathan Glazer *Cinematography* Harris Savides *Production Design* Kevin Thompson *Costumes* John A. Dunn *Editing* Sam Sneade and Claus Wehlisch *Music* Alexandre Desplat *Production* Lizie Gower, Nick Morris and Jean-Louis Piel *Cast* Nicole Kidman (Anna), Cameron Bright (Young Sean), Danny Huston (Joseph), Lauren Bacall (Eleanor).

### Chanel No.5: The Film (short)
*Direction* Baz Luhrmann *Cinematography* Mandy Walker *Editing* Daniel Schwarze *Music* Craig Armstrong (arrangement) *Production* Baz Luhrmann *Cast* Nicole Kidman and Rodrigo Santoro.

## 2005
### The Interpreter
*Direction* Sydney Pollack *Screenplay* Scott Frank, Charles Randolph and Steven Zaillian, from a story by Martin Stellman and Brian Ward *Cinematography* Darius Khondji *Production Design* Jon Hutman *Costumes* Sarah Edwards *Editing* William Steinkamp *Music* James Newton Howard *Production* Tim Bevan, Eric Fellner and Kevin Misher *Cast* Nicole Kidman (Silvia Broome), Sean Penn (Tobin Keller), Catherine Keener (Dot Woods), Yvan Attal (Philippe).

### Bewitched
*Direction* Nora Ephron *Screenplay* Nora Ephron and Delia Ephron, from the TV series by Sol Saks *Cinematography* John Lindley *Production Design* Neil Spisak *Costumes* Mary Zophres *Editing* Tia Nolan *Music* George Fenton *Production* Nora Ephron, Lucy Fischer, Penny Marshall and Douglas Wick *Cast* Nicole Kidman (Isabel Bigelow/Samantha), Will Ferrell (Jack Wyatt/Darrin), Shirley MacLaine (Iris Smythson/Endora), Michael Caine (Nigel Bigelow), Jason Schwartzman (Ritchie).

## 2006
### Fur: An Imaginary Portrait of Diane Arbus
*Direction* Steven Shainberg *Screenplay* Erin Cressida Wilson, from a book by Patricia Bosworth *Cinematography* Bill Pope *Production Design* Amy Danger *Costumes* Mark Bridges *Editing* Kristina Boden and Keiko Deguchi *Music* Carter Burwell *Production* Laura Bickford, Andrew Fierberg, Bill Pohlad and Bonnie Timmermann *Cast* Nicole Kidman (Diane Arbus), Robert Downey Jr (Lionel Sweeney), Ty Burrell (Allan Arbus), Harris Yulin (David Nemerov).

### Happy Feet
*Direction* George Miller, Warren Coleman and Judy Morris *Screenplay* George Miller, John Collee, Judy Morris and Warren Coleman *Cinematography* David Peers *Production Design* Mark Sexton *Editing* Christian Gazal and Margaret Sixel *Music* John Powell *Production* Bill Miller, George Miller and Doug Mitchell *Cast* the voices of Elijah Wood (Mumble), Brittany Murphy (Gloria), Hugh Jackman (Memphis), Nicole Kidman (Norma Jean), Robin Williams (Ramon/Lovelace).

## 2007
### The Invasion
*Direction* Oliver Hirschbiegel and James McTeigue (uncredited) *Screenplay* David Kajganich, from the novel *The Body Snatchers* by Jack Finney *Cinematography* Rainer Klausmann *Production Design* Jack Fisk *Costumes* Jacqueline West *Music* John Ottman *Production* Joel Silver *Cast* Nicole Kidman (Carol Bennell), Daniel Craig (Ben Driscoll), Jeremy Northam (Tucker Kaufman).

### Margot at the Wedding
*Direction* Noah Baumbach *Screenplay* Noah Baumbach *Cinematography* Harris Savides *Production Design* Anne Ross *Costumes* Ann Roth *Editing* Carol Littleton *Production* Scott Rudin *Cast* Nicole Kidman (Margot), Jack Black (Malcolm), Jennifer Jason Leigh (Pauline).

### The Golden Compass
*Direction* Chris Weitz *Screenplay* Chris Weitz, from the novel *Northern Lights* by Philip Pullman *Cinematography* Henry Braham *Production Design* Dennis Gassner *Costumes* Ruth Myers *Editing* Anne V. Coates, Peter Honess and Kevin Tent *Music* Alexandre Desplat *Production* Bill Carraro *Cast* Nicole Kidman (Marisa Coulter), Daniel Craig (Lord Asriel), Dakota Blue Richards (Lyra), Ben Walker (Roger).

## 2008
### Australia
*Direction* Baz Luhrmann *Screenplay* Stuart Beattie, Baz Luhrmann, Richard Flanagan and Ronald Harwood, from a story by Baz Luhrmann *Cinematography* Mandy Walker *Production Design* Catherine Martin *Costumes* Catherine Martin *Editing* Dody Dorn and Michael McCusker *Music* David Hirschfelder *Production* G. Mac Brown, Catherine Knapman and Baz Luhrmann *Cast* Nicole Kidman (Lady Sarah Ashley), Hugh Jackman (Drover), David Wenham (Neil Fletcher), Bryan Brown (Lesley 'King' Carney), Jack Thompson (Kipling Flynn), David Gulpilil (King George), Brandon Walters (Nullah), David Ngoombujarra (Magarri), Ben Mendelsohn (Captain Emmett Dutton), Essie Davis (Catherine 'Cath' Carney Fletcher), Barry Otto (Administrator Allsop), Kerry Walker (Myrtle Alsop), Sandy Gore (Gloria Carney), Ursula Yovich (Daisy), Lillian Crombie (Bandy Legs).

## 2009
### Nine
*Direction* Rob Marshall *Screenplay* Michael Tolkin, Anthony Minghella, from the Italian musical by Mario Fratti, adapted for Broadway by Arthur Kopit and Maury Yeston *Cinematography* Dion Beebe *Production Design* John Myhre *Costumes* Colleen Atwood *Editing* Claire Simpson and Wyatt Smith *Music* Andrea Guerra *Production* John DeLuca, Rob Marshall, Marc Platt and Harvey Weinstein *Cast* Daniel Day-Lewis (Guido Contini), Nicole Kidman (Claudia),

Marion Cotillard (Luisa Contini), Penélope Cruz (Carla), Judi Dench (Lilli), Sophia Loren (Mamma).

## 2010
### Rabbit Hole
*Direction* John Cameron Mitchell *Screenplay* David Lindsay-Abaire, from his own play *Cinematography* Frank G. DeMarco *Production Design* Kalina Ivanov *Costumes* Ann Roth *Editing* Joe Klotz *Music* Anton Sanko *Production* Nicole Kidman, Gigi Pritzker, Per Saari, Leslie Urdang and Dean Vanech *Cast* Nicole Kidman (Becca), Aaron Eckhart (Howie), Dianne Wiest (Nat), Miles Teller (Jason).

## 2011
### Just Go with It
*Direction* Dennis Dugan *Screenplay* Allan Leob and Timothy Dowling *Cinematography* Theo van de Sande *Production Design* Perry Andelin Blake *Editing* Tom Costain *Music* Rupert Gregson-Williams *Production* Jack Giarraputo, Heather Parry and Adam Sandler *Cast* Adam Sandler (Danny), Jennifer Aniston (Katherine), Nicole Kidman (Devlin Adams).

### Trespass
*Direction* Joel Schumacher *Screenplay* Karl Gajdusek *Cinematography* Andrzej Bartkowiak *Production Design* Nathan Amondson *Costumes* Judianna Makovsky *Editing* Bill Pankow *Music* David Buckley *Production* René Besson, David Winkler and Irwin Winkler *Cast* Nicolas Cage (Kyle Miller), Nicole Kidman (Sarah Miller), Ben Mendelsohn (Elias), Liana Liberato (Avery Miller).

## 2012
### The Paperboy
*Direction* Lee Daniels *Screenplay* Peter Dexter and Lee Daniels, from the novel by

Peter Dexter *Cinematography* Robert Schaefer *Production Design* Daniel T. Dorrance *Costumes* Caroline Eselin *Editing* Joe Klotz *Music* Mario Grigorov *Production* Ed Cathell III, Lee Daniels, Cassian Elwes, Avi Lerner and Hilary Shor *Cast* Zac Efron (Jack Jansen), Matthew McConaughey (Ward Jansen), Nicole Kidman (Charlotte Bless), John Cusack (Hillary Van Wetter), David Oyelowo (Yardley Acheman), Scott Glenn (W. W. Jansen).

### Hemingway & Gellhorn (TV)
*Direction* Philip Kaufman *Screenplay* Jerry Stahl and Barbara Turner *Cinematography* Rogier Stoffers *Production Design* Geoffrey Kirkland *Costumes* Ruth Myers *Editing* Walter Murch *Music* Javier Navarrete *Production* James Gandolfini, Peter Kaufman, Barbara Turner. With Nicole Kidman (Martha Gellhorn), Clive Owen (Ernest Hemingway), David Strathairn (John Dos Passos).

## 2013
### Stoker
*Direction* Park Chan-wook *Screenplay* Wentworth Miller *Cinematography* Chung Chung-hoon *Production Design* Thérèse DePrez *Costumes* Kurt and Bart *Editing* Nicolas De Toth *Music* Clint Mansell *Production* Michael Costigan, Ridley Scott and Tony Scott *Cast* Mia Wasikowska (India Stoker), Nicole Kidman (Evelyn Stoker), David Alford (Reverend), Matthew Goode (Charles Stoker).

### The Railway Man
*Direction* Jonathan Teplitzky *Screenplay* Frank Cottrell Boyce and Andy Paterson, from the book by Eric Lomax *Cinematography* Garry Phillips *Production Design* Steven Jones-Evans *Costumes* Lizzy Gardiner *Editing* Martin Connor *Music* David

Hirschfelder *Production* Chris Brown, Bill Curbishley and Andy Paterson *Cast* Jeremy Irvine (Young Eric), Colin Firth (Eric), Stellan Skarsgård (Finlay), Nicole Kidman (Patti).

## 2014
### Grace of Monaco
*Direction* Olivier Dahan *Screenplay* Arash Amel *Cinematography* Eric Gautier *Production Design* Dan Weil *Costumes* Gigi Lepage *Editing* Olivier Gajan *Music* Christopher Gunning *Production* Uday Chopra and Arash Amel *Cast* Nicole Kidman (Grace Kelly), Tim Roth (Rainier III), Frank Langella (Father Francis Tucker), Parker Posey (Madge Tivey-Faucon).

### Before I Go to Sleep
*Direction* Rowan Joffé *Screenplay* Rowan Joffé, from the novel by S.J. Watson *Cinematography* Ben Davis *Production Design* Kave Quinn *Costumes* Michele Clapton *Editing* Melanie Oliver *Music* Edward Shearmur *Production* Mark Gill, Avi Lerner and Ridley Scott *Cast* Nicole Kidman (Christine), Colin Firth (Mike), Mark Strong (Dr Nasch), Anne-Marie Duff (Claire).

### Paddington
*Direction* Paul King *Screenplay* Paul King and Hamish McColl, based on the character created by Michael Bond *Cinematography* Erik Wilson *Production Design* Gary Williamson *Costumes* Lindy Hemming *Editing* Mark Everson *Music* Nick Urata *Production* David Heyman *Cast* Ben Whishaw (Paddington, voice), Hugh Bonneville (Henry Brown), Sally Hawkins (Mary Brown), Julie Walters (Mrs Bird), Jim Broadbent (Samuel Gruber), Peter Capaldi (Reginald Curry), Nicole Kidman (Millicent).

### Hello Ladies: The Movie (TV)
*Direction* Stephen Merchant *Screenplay* Stephen Merchant, Gene Stupnitsky and Lee Eisenberg *Cinematography* Michael A. Price *Production Design* Jim Wallis *Costumes* Susan Michalek *Editing* Justin Bourret *Music* Vik Sharma *Production* Dan Kaplow *Cast* Stephen Merchant (Stuart), Christine Woods (Jessica), Nate Torrence (Wade), Kevin Weisman (Kives), Nicole Kidman (as herself).

## 2015
### Strangerland
*Direction* Kim Farrant *Screenplay* Michael Kinirons and Fiona Seres *Cinematography* P. J. Dillon *Production Design* Melinda Doring *Costumes* Emily Seresin *Editing* Veronika Jenet *Music* Keefus Ciancia *Production* Macdara Kelleher and Naomi Wenck *Cast* Nicole Kidman (Catherine Parker), Joseph Fiennes (Matthew Parker), Hugo Weaving (David Rae).

### Queen of the Desert
*Direction* Werner Herzog *Screenplay* Werner Herzog *Cinematography* Peter Zeitlinger *Production Design* Ulrich Bergfelder *Costumes* Michele Clapton *Editing* Joe Bini *Music* Klaus Badelt *Production* Michael Benaroya, Cassian Elwes and Nick N. Raslan *Cast* Nicole Kidman (Gertrude Bell), James Franco (Henry Cadogan), Robert Pattinson (Col. T. E. Lawrence).

### The Family Fang
*Direction* Jason Bateman *Screenplay* David Lindsay-Abaire, from the novel by Kevin Wilson *Cinematography* Ken Seng *Production Design* Beth Mickle *Costumes* Amy Westcott *Editing* Robert Frazen *Music* Carter Burwell *Production* Jason Bateman, James Garavente, Nicole Kidman, Riva Marker,

Per Saari, Daniela Taplin
Lundberg, Leslie Urdang
and Dean Vanech *Cast*
Jason Bateman (Buster Fang),
Nicole Kidman (Annie Fang),
Christopher Walken
(Caleb Fang), Marin Ireland
(Suzanne Crosby).

## Genius
*Direction* Michael Grandage
*Screenplay* John Logan, from
the novel by A. Scott Berg
*Cinematography* Ben Davis
*Production Design* Mark
Digby *Costumes* Jane Petrie
*Editing* Chris Dickens *Music*
Adam Cork *Production*
James Bierman, Michael
Grandage and John Logan
*Cast* Colin Firth (Max
Perkins), Nicole Kidman
(Aline Bernstein), Jude Law
(Thomas Wolfe), Guy Pearce
(F. Scott Fitzgerald).

## Secret in Their Eyes
*Direction* Billy Ray
*Screenplay* Billy Ray, from
the novel by Eduardo Sacheri
*Cinematography* Daniel
Moder *Production Design*
Nelson Coates *Costumes*
Shay Cunliffe *Music* Emilio
Kauderer *Production* Matt
Jackson and Mark Johnson
*Cast* Nicole Kidman (Claire),
Julia Roberts (Jess), Chiwetel
Ejiofor (Ray).

# Bibliography

*Articles*

Samuel Blumenfeld, 'Nicole
    Kidman à corps perdu',
    *Le Monde*,
    14 September 2012.
Olivier Bonnard, 'Portrait de
    femme', *Le Nouvel Obs*,
    14 April 2011.
Laurent Bouzereau,
    'Entretien avec Nicole
    Kidman', *L'Écran
    fantastique*, July 1995.
Michel Ciment and Yann
    Tobin, 'Entretien
    avec Nicole Kidman',
    *Positif*, summer 2012.
Florence Colombani,
    'Nicole Kidman au pays
    de la douleur', *Le Point*,
    14 April 2014.
Pam Cook, 'Who Does Nicole
    Kidman Undress in the
    Opening Shot of *Eyes Wide
    Shut*?', *Fashion into Film*,
    23 March 2012.
Emma Cox, 'Nicole Kidman
    Interview', *Daily Mail*,
    8 December 2012.
Leslie Felperin, 'Nicole
    Kidman Interview',
    *The Guardian*,
    26 December 2013.
Emmanuelle Frois, 'Kidman:
    J'aime personnellement
    m'engager', *Le Figaro*,
    19 March 2003.
Agnès Peck, 'Quatre visages
    de Nicole Kidman',
    *Positif*, January 2002.
Fabrice Pliskin, '*Prête à tout*',
    *Le Nouvel Obs*,
    7 December 1995.
Denis Rossano, '*Moulin
    Rouge*', *L'Express*, 10 May
    2001.
Marianne Ruuth and Jean-
    Luc Wachthausen, 'Nicole
    Kidman mène la revue',
    *Le Figaro*, 9 May 2001.

*Books*

Susan Batson, *Truth:
    Personas, Needs, and Flaws
    in the Art of Building
    Actors and Creating
    Characters*, New York, NY:
    Rugged Land Books, 2007.
Pam Cook, *Nicole Kidman*,
    London: BFI Publishing,
    2012.
James L. Dickerson, *Nicole
    Kidman*, Brandon, MS:
    Sartoris Literary Group,
    2014.
Marie Lherault, *Nicole
    Kidman*, Paris: Nouveau
    Monde Éditions, 2010.
Jeffrey Robinson, *Princesse
    Grace*, Neuilly-sur-Seine:
    Michel Lafon, 2014.
Caterina Rossi, *Nicole
    Kidman*, Milan: L'Epos,
    2011.
David Thomson, *Nicole
    Kidman*, London:
    Bloomsbury, 2006.

## Notes

1   David Thomson, *Nicole Kidman*, Bloomsbury, London, 2006, p. 16.
2   *Ibid.*, p. 31.
3   *Ibid.*
4   Pam Cook, 'Nicole Kidman: What a Performance', lecture at the University of Southampton, 15 November 2011.
5   Paul Auster, *The Red Notebook*, Faber & Faber, 1995.
6   Pam Cook, *Nicole Kidman*, BFI Palgrave Macmillan, London, 2012.
7   Barbara Théate, 'Nicole Kidman en poupée russe', *Le Journal du Dimanche*, 3 August 2003.
8   Michel Ciment and Yann Tobin, 'Entretien avec Nicole Kidman', *Positif*, summer 2012.
9   *Ibid.*, p. 25.
10  Roland Barthes, *Mythologies* (1957), Œuvres complètes, Seuil, Paris, 1993, pp. 604–5.
11  Stéphane Bouquet and Jean-Marc Lalanne, *Gus Van Sant*, Cahiers du cinéma, Paris, 2009, p. 86.
12  Michel Serres (tr. Randolph Burkes), *Statues: The Second Book of Foundations* (1987), Bloomsbury Academic, London, 2015.
13  Tarik Khaldi, *Official Website* of the *Festival de Cannes*, 25 May 2013.
14  Shown in the documentary *Orson Welles: The One-Man Band* (1995),

available on some DVD editions of *F for Fake*.
15  Leslie Felperin, 'Nicole Kidman: "I Try Never to Be Governed by Fear"', *The Guardian*, 26 December 2013.
16  Kidman at *Paperboy* press conference, Cannes Film Festival, 24 May 2012.
17  Thomson, *op. cit.*, p. 37.
18  Marie Lherault, *Nicole Kidman*, Nouveau Monde, Paris, 2010, p. 26.
19  Arthur Rimbaud (tr. Dennis J. Carlile), *The Works*, Xlibris, Bloomington, IN, 2000.
20  Lherault, *op. cit.*, pp. 26–7.
21  Cook, *op. cit.*
22  Emma Cox, 'Interview: Nicole Kidman', *Daily Mail*, 8 December 2012.
23  Variety Staff, 'Dead Calm', *Variety*, 31 December 1988.
24  Rita Kempley, '*Dead Calm*', *Washington Post*, 7 April 1989.
25  Thomson, *op. cit.*, p. 39.
26  Cook, *op. cit.*
27  'Prête à tout', *France Soir*, 23 May 1995.
28  Thomson, *op. cit.*, p. 79.
29  *Ibid.*, p. 75.
30  The main title sequence, which is like a character study, was created by designer Pablo Ferro, known for his exploration of the faces of Faye Dunaway and Steve McQueen in the split-screen credits for *The Thomas Crown Affair* (1968).

31  Cook, *op. cit.*
32  Bouquet and Lalanne, *op. cit.*, p. 80.
33  *Ibid.*, p. 82.
34  *Ibid.*, p. 84.
35  *Ibid.*, p. 86.
36  Fabrice Pliskin, '*Prête à tout*', *Le Nouvel Obs*, 7 December 1995.
37  'Prête à tout', *France Soir*, 23 May 1995.
38  Valérie Duponchelle, '*Prête à tout*', *Le Figaro*, 22 May 1995.
39  Michael Wilmington, '*To Die For*', *Chicago Tribune*, 6 October 1995.
40  Stéphane Bouquet, 'Trop de désir tue', *Cahiers du cinéma*, December 1995.
41  Pliskin, *op. cit.*
42  Cook, *op. cit.*
43  Peter Long and Kate Ellis (directors), *The Making of 'The Portrait of a Lady'* (DVD), Universal, 1997.
44  Ciment and Tobin, *op. cit.*
45  Marie-Elisabeth Rouchy, '*Portrait de femme*', *Télérama*, 18 December 1996.
46  *Ibid.*
47  Long and Ellis, *op. cit.*
48  Lherault, *op. cit*, p. 67.
49  *Ibid.*
50  Michel Ciment, *Jane Campion by Jane Campion*, Cahiers du cinéma, Paris, 2014, p. 113.
51  Rouchy, *op. cit.*
52  Simone de Beauvoir, *The Second Sex* (1949) (tr. H. M. Parshley), Penguin Books, Harmondsworth, 1972.
53  Thomson, *op. cit.*, p. 96.
54  *Ibid.*, p. 85.

55  Rouchy, *op. cit.*
56  Claude Baignères, '*Portrait de femme*', *Le Figaro*, 18 December 1996.
57  Barbara Shulgasser, '*Portrait of a Lady*', *San Francisco Examiner*, 17 January 1997.
58  Agnès Peck, 'Quatre visages de Nicole Kidman', *Positif*, January 2002.
59  Olivier Bonnard, '*Portrait de femme*', *Le Nouvel Obs*, 14 April 2011.
60  Nicole Kidman, *Kidman on Kubrick*, bonus DVD to *Eyes Wide Shut*, Warner Home Video, 2000.
61  *Ibid.*
62  *Ibid.*
63  Samuel Blumenfeld, 'Nicole Kidman à corps perdu', *Le Monde*, 15 September 2012.
64  *Kidman on Kubrick*, *op. cit.*
65  *Ibid.*
66  Pam Cook, 'Why Does Nicole Kidman Undress in the Opening Shot of *Eyes Wide Shut*?', *Fashion into Film*, 23 March 2012.
67  *Ibid.*
68  Blumenfeld, 'Nicole Kidman à corps perdu', *op. cit.*
69  Edgar Morin, *Les Stars*, Editions du Seuil, Paris, 1972, p. 180.
70  Jean-Michel Frodon, 'Une version française signée Pascale Ferran', *Le Monde*, 15 September 1999.
71  *Kidman on Kubrick*, *op. cit.*

72 Michael Wilmington, 'The Sexy, Scary, Stylish *Eyes Wide Shut* Is Stanley Kubrick's Final Masterpiece', *Chicago Tribune*, 16 July 1999.

73 Joan Smith, 'Pornography or Art? What the Billboards Don't Tell You About Stanley Kubrick's Last Film, *Eyes Wide Shut*', *The Independent*, 18 July 1999.

74 François Gorin, '*Eyes Wide Shut*', *Télérama*, 21 July 1999.

75 Philippe Garnier, 'Venise ouvre l'œil. La Mostra démarre avec *Eyes Wide Shut* de Kubrick', *Libération*, 1 September 1999.

76 Peck, *op. cit.*

77 Blumenfeld, 'Nicole Kidman à corps perdu', *op. cit.*

78 Patrick Amory, 'Christiane Kubrick', *Paris Match*, 9 September 1999.

79 Marianne Ruuth and Jean-Luc Wachthausen, 'Nicole Kidman mène la revue', *Le Figaro*, 9 May 2001.

80 Denis Rossano, 'Nicole Kidman les yeux grands ouverts', *L'Express*, 10 May 2001.

81 Lherault, *op. cit*, p. 97.

82 Ruuth and Wachthausen, *op. cit.*

83 *Ibid.*

84 Rossano, *op. cit.*

85 Peck, *op. cit.*

86 *Ibid.*

87 Nicole Kidman, *Moulin Rouge!* press conference, Cannes Film Festival, 9 May 2001.

88 Rossano, *op. cit.*

89 Quoted by Mathilde Blottière, 'Cannes et les Américains (5/5)', *Télérama*, 10 May 2013.

90 Samuel Blumenfeld, 'Un délire trop orchestré', *Le Monde*, 3 October 2001.

91 Olivier Père, 'Diamant dans écrin toc', *Les Inrockuptibles*, 3 October 2001.

92 Peck, *op. cit.*

93 Neil Smith, 'Movies: *Moulin Rouge!*', *BBC.com*, 22 June 2001.

94 Michael Charlton, 'Performing Gender in the Studio and Postmodern Musical', *Alphaville: Journal of Film and Screen Media*, issue 3, summer 2012.

95 Thomson, *op. cit.*, p. 151.

96 *Ibid.*, p. 168.

97 *Ibid.*

98 Samuel Blumenfeld, '*Les Autres* : les morts-vivants sont toujours aussi terrifiants', *Le Monde*, 26 December 2001.

99 *Ibid.*

100 Pascal Quignard, 'Petit Traité sur Méduse', in *Le Nom sur le bout de la langue*, Gallimard, Paris, 1995, p. 90.

101 Thomson, *op. cit.*, pp. 171–2.

102 J. M. G. Le Clézio, *Mydriase* (1973), published together with *Vers les icebergs*, Mercure de France, Paris, 2014, p. 44.

103 *Ibid.*, pp. 20–1.

104 Peck, *op. cit.*

105 Marianne Ruuth, 'Imprévisible Nicole Kidman', *Le Figaro*, 26 December 2001.

106 A. O. Scott, 'Which of You People Are the Dead Ones?', *The New York Times*, 10 August 2001.

107 Amy Taubin, 'The Shinings', *The Village Voice*, 7 August 2001.

108 Wesley Morris, 'Film Clips: *The Others*', *San Francisco Chronicle*, 10 August 2001.

109 Jean-Pierre Dufreigne, 'Le Goût des autres', *L'Express*, 27 Dec. 2001.

110 Peck, *op. cit.*

111 Blumenfeld, 'Nicole Kidman à corps perdu', *op. cit.*

112 Emmanuelle Frois, 'Kidman: j'aime personnellement m'engager', *Le Figaro*, 19 March 2003.

113 Laure Becdelièvre, 'Virginia Woolf, Nicole Kidman et *The Hours*: de la vérité d'un faux nez', *Le Huffington Post*, 15 June 2012.

114 DVD audio commentary, *The Hours*, Paramount, 2003.

115 Frois, *op. cit.*

116 *Ibid.*

117 Richard Gianorio, 'Nicole Kidman a du nez', *France Soir*, 19 March 2003.

118 Blumenfeld, 'Nicole Kidman à corps perdu', *op. cit.*

119 Becdelièvre, *op. cit.*

120 Virginia Woolf, 'The Cinema', *The Arts*, New York, June 1926.

121 Becdelièvre, *op. cit.*

122 Morin, *op. cit*, p. 41

123 *Ibid.*, p. 43

124 Thomson, *op. cit*, pp. 171–80.

125 DVD audio commentary, *op. cit.*

126 Thomson, *op. cit.*, p. 180.

127 *Ibid.*

128 Gérard Lefort, 'Kidman en Virginia Woolf: chapeau!', *Libération*, 10 February 2003.

129 Pascal Mérigeau, 'Actrices', *Le Nouvel Obs*, 20 March 2003.

130 Gianorio, *op. cit.*

131 Peter Travers, '*The Hours*', *Rolling Stone*, 24 January 2003.

132 Stephen Holden, 'Who's Afraid Like Virginia Woolf?', *The New York Times*, 27 December 2002.

133 Patricia Cohen, 'The Virginia Woolf of *The Hours* Angers the Real One's Fans', *The New York Times*, 15 February 2003.

134 Brenda R. Silver, *Virginia Woolf Icon*, The University of Chicago Press, Chicago, 1999.

135 DVD audio commentary, *op. cit.*

136 Frois, *op. cit.*

137 Thomas Sotinel, 'Je suis dépendante de Lars von Trier', *Le Monde*, 21 May 2003.

138 'Lars von Trier déjà favori avec *Dogville*', *Le Journal du Dimanche*, 18 May 2003.

139 Nicole Kidman, '*Dogville* Q&A', *Nicolekidmanofficial.com*, 20 December 2011.

140 *Ibid.*

141 Marie-Noëlle Tranchant, 'Lars von Trier dans le train de la vengeance', *Le Figaro*, 19 May 2003.

142 Kidman, *op. cit.*

143 Sotinel, *op. cit.*

144 Jean-Michel Frodon, 'Entretien Lars von Trier', *Le Monde*, 15 May 2003.

145 Blumenfeld, 'Nicole Kidman à corps perdu', *op. cit.*

146 Olivier Bonnard, '*Rabbit Hole*', *Le Nouvel Obs*, 14 April 2011.

147 'Lars von Trier déjà favori avec *Dogville*', *op. cit.*

148 Louis Guichard, '*Dogville*', *Télérama*, 21 May 2003.

149 Peter Baechlin, *Histoire économique du cinéma*, La Nouvelle Edition, Paris, 1947, p. 172.

150 Morin, *op. cit.*, pp. 41–3.

151 Michel Foucault, *Discipline & Punishment: The Birth of the Prison* (tr. Alan Sheridan), Random House, New York, 1995. (Originally published in 1975 as *Surveiller et Punir: Naissance de la prison* by Gallimard, Paris.)

152 Alexandre Georgandas, 'Dans la tête de Trier', *Cadrage*, April 2012.

153 Kidman, *op. cit.*

154 *Ibid.*

155 *Ibid.*

156 Todd McCarthy, 'Review: *Dogville*', *Variety*, 19 May 2003.

157 Thomson, *op. cit.*

158 J. Hoberman, 'The Grace of Wrath', *Village Voice*, 16 March 2004.

159 Guichard, *op. cit.*

160 Olivier de Bruyn, 'Nicole Kidman: Cannes lui

appartient', *Le Point*, 23 May 2003.

161 Roger Ebert, '*Dogville*', *Chicago Tribune*, 9 April 2004.

162 Olivier Bonnard, '*Rabbit Hole*', *Le Nouvel Obs*, 14 April 2011.

163 Léna Lutaud, 'Nicole Kidman produit son premier film à New York', *Le Figaro*, 4 September 2009.

164 Florence Colombani, 'Nicole Kidman au pays de la douleur', *Le Point*, 14 April 2011.

165 *Ibid.*

166 'Aaron Eckhart Says He Argued with Nicole Kidman on Set of *Rabbit Hole*', *The Huffington Post*, 21 December 2010.

167 '*Rabbit Hole*'s Miles Teller on Acting with Nicole Kidman', *Blackbook*, 17 December 2010.

168 Bonus DVD, *Rabbit Hole*, Lionsgate, 2011.

169 *Ibid.*

170 *Ibid.*

171 Tom Charity, 'Review: Kidman Shines in Painfully Honest *Rabbit Hole*', *CNN*, 17 December 2010.

172 Léo Soesanto, 'Nicole Kidman remarquable dans *Rabbit Hole*', *Les Inrocks*, 12 April 2011.

173 *Ibid.*

174 S.T. Van Airsdale, 'John Cameron Mitchell on *Rabbit Hole*, Nicole Kidman's Face and How to Share Power on the Set', *Movieline*, 16 September 2010.

175 Emma Cox, 'Nicole Kidman: "It's Important to Do Things That Scare You"', *The Mail on Sunday*, 8 December 2012.

176 Bonus DVD, *op. cit.*

177 Béla Balázs, *Theory of the Film: Character and Growth of a New Art* (1948) (tr. Edith Bone), Dennis Dobson Ltd, London, 1952, p. 288.

178 Morin, *op. cit.*, pp. 41–3.

179 Bonnard, *op. cit.*

180 Colombani, *op. cit.*

181 Louis Guichard, '*Rabbit Hole*', *Télérama*, 13 April 2011.

182 Peter Travers, '*Rabbit Hole*', *Rolling Stone*, 16 December 2010.

183 Roger Ebert, '*Rabbit Hole*', *Chicago Sun-Times*, 22 Dec. 2010.

184 Charity, *op. cit.*

185 'Marion Cotillard on Nicole Kidman in *Rabbit Hole*', *Variety*, 29 November 2010.

186 Bonnard, *op. cit.*

187 Caroline Vié, 'Nicole Kidman: "Je sais ce que c'est que de vivre dans une cage dorée"', *20 Minutes*, 13 May 2014.

188 Alain Grasset, 'Nicole Kidman: "Moi aussi, j'ai vécu dans une cage dorée…"', *Le Parisien*, 14 May 2014.

189 Bonus DVD, *Grace de Monaco*, TF1 Vidéo, 2014.

190 *Grace of Monaco* press conference, Cap d'Antibes, 14 May 2014.

191 Michael Cieply, 'A Hollywood Princess Returns to the Screen', *The New York Times*, 13 May 2014.

192 Danielle Attali, 'Olivier Dahan: "Je revendique le droit à la fiction"', *Le Journal du Dimanche*, 19 January 2013.

193 Grasset, *op. cit.*

194 Steven Zeitchik, 'Cannes 2014: *Grace of Monaco* Opening More Awkward Than Regal', *LA Times*, 14 May 2014.

195 Thomas Perillon, '*Grace de Monaco* avec Nicole Kidman: l'erreur de casting d'un film ennuyeux et raté', *Le Nouvel Obs*, 15 May 2014.

196 Scott Foundas, 'Cannes Film Review: *Grace of Monaco*', *Variety*, 14 May 2014.

197 Eric Kohn, 'Cannes Review: Nicole Kidman Is a Solid Grace Kelly in *Grace of Monaco*, but Is It Fact or Fiction?', *Indiewire*, 14 May 2014.

198 Cook, *Nicole Kidman*, *op. cit.*

199 Vié, *op. cit.*

200 Jérôme Vermelin, 'Nicole Kidman: "J'aimerais rencontrer les enfants de Grace de Monaco"', *Metronews*, 14 May 2014.

201 Olivier Bonnard, 'Nicole Kidman: "Plus on essaie de me brider, et plus ça me donne envie de ruer dans les brancards"', *Le Nouvel Obs*, 24 May 2012.

202 Serres, *op. cit.*

*Sidebar Notes*

a Michel Ciment and Yann Tobin, *op. cit.*

b *Ibid.*

c *Ibid.*

d *Ibid.*

e Michel Ciment, *Jane Campion by Jane Campion*, Cahiers du cinéma, Paris, 2014, pp. 182–3.

f Samuel Blumenfeld, 'Nicole Kidman, croquée toute crue', *Le Monde*, 26 May 2012.

g Olivier Bonnard, 'Nicole Kidman, prête à tout', *Le Nouvel Obs*, 17 October 2012.

h Samuel Blumenfeld, 'Nicole Kidman à corps perdu', *op. cit.*

i Jean-Marc Lalanne, '*Ma sorcière bien-aimée*', *Les Inrocks*, 21 September 2005.

j Peter Debruge, 'Berlin Film Review: *Queen of the Desert*', *Variety*, 6 February 2015.

k Thomas Sotinel, '*Fur* de Steven Shainberg', *Le Monde*, 12 January 2007.

l Louis Guichard, '*Fur: un portrait imaginaire de Diane Arbus*', *Télérama*, 10 January 2007.

m C. D.-M., 'L'expiation de Nicole Kidman', *Marianne*, 6 January 2007.

Numbers in *italics* refer to illustrations.

*A Cry in the Dark* 29
*The Accused* 29
Adams, Amy 155
Affleck, Casey 33, *35*
Aguirresarobe, Javier 101
*Alice in Wonderland* 67, 156
Amenábar, Alejandro 7, 13, 84, 95, 101, 104
Andersson, Harriet *126, 127*
Apted, Michael 29
Arquette, Patricia 33
Ashton-Griffiths, Roger 156, *158-9*
Auster, Paul 12
*Australia* 44, 136, 139, 148, *172-3*, 176
*The Aviator* 171
Bacall, Lauren 12, 20, *126, 127*
Bailey, Fenton 12
*Bangkok Hilton* 31, *174*
Barbato, Randy 12
Barthes, Roland 17
*Basic Instinct* 66
*Batman Forever* 33, *174, 175*
*Batman Returns* 171
Baumbach, Noah 44
Beaton, Cecil 119
*Before I Go to Sleep* 13
*Bell, Book and Candle* 38
Bentley, James *94, 95*
Benton, Robert 8-9, 29, 33, 66, *118-9, 174, 175*
Bergman, Ingmar 127
Bergman, Ingrid 134
Bettany, Paul *127, 130*
*Bewitched* 44, 60, 81, 105, 136, 175, *178*
*Billy Bathgate* 33, 66, 118, 175
*Birth* 12-13, 44, 136, 140, 144, 148, 152, 175
*Birthday Girl* 13, *16*, 44, 66, 175
Björk 123, *131*
Blanchett, Cate 8, 171
Blossom Films 139, 176
*The Blue Angel* 80, 81
*The Blue Room* 64, 76, 175
Blumenfeld, Samuel 66, 76, 89
*BMX Bandits* 6, 8, 175
Bovary, Emma 38

Brando, Marlon 25
Broadbent, Jim 81
Brontë (sisters) 109, 112
Burton, Tim 171
*Bush Christmas* 8, 175
Butterworth, Jez 13, *16*, 44, 66
Caan, James 127, *135*
*Cabaret* 80, 81
Cameron Mitchell, John 13, 44, 139, *150-1*
Campion, Jane 7, 13, 44, *45, 47, 49, 50, 54, 55*, 58, *59, 61*, 171, 175
*Catch-22* 33
Cervi, Valentina *52-3*
Chan-wook, Park *10-11*, 12, 44, 148, *177*
Chaplin, Ben 66
*Chicago* 171
Clarkson, Patricia *134*
Close, Glenn 29
*Cold Mountain* 8, 44, 119, *189*
Cook, Pam 8, 25, 31, 34, 42, 64, 70, 168
Costner, Kevin 20
Cotillard, Marion 152
Craig, Daniel 12
Cruise, Tom 12, *14-15*, 31, 33, 42, *63-4, 65, 72-3*, 76, 95, 115, 131, 148, 175
Cunningham, Michael 109
Cusack, John 66
Dahan, Olivier 13, 95, 155, 160, 168, 176
Daldry, Stephen 13, 109, 112, *120-1*, 171
*Dancer in the Dark* 123, *134*
*Dances with Wolves* 20
*Dangerous Liaisons* 29
Daniels, Lee 12-13, 44, 66, 105, 176
*Days of Thunder* 31, 33, *174, 175*
De Beauvoir, Simone 58
De Gaulle, Charles *165, 169*
*Dead Calm* 13, 17, *18, 19-20, 21-4, 25, 26-7*, 29-30, 66, 97, 101, 144, 148, 168, 175
*The Deep* 19

Deneuve, Catherine 136, 171
*Diamonds Are a Girl's Best Friend* 81, 92
Dietrich, Marlene 81, 92
Dillane, Stephen *110*
Dillon, Matt 33, *36-7, 175*
*Dogville* 12-13, 44, 66, 105, 119, 122, 123, *124-33, 134, 135, 136, 137*, 148-9, 175
Donovan, Martin 58
Du Mont, Sky 65
Duigan, John 7, 8, 79
Dulac, Germaine 50
Dunne, Griffin 8, 105
Duvall, Shelley 60
Ebert, Roger 136, 149
Eckhart, Aaron 139, *141, 142-3*
Efron, Zac 66
Eginton, Madison *68-9*
Eliot, George 7, 109
*Emerald City* 8, 31
Ephron, Nora 13, 44, 81, 105, 136, 171, 175, *178*
Eurydice 85, 89, 144
*Eyes Wide Shut* 13, 62, *64-5*, 66, *67-75*, 76, *77*, 85, 89, 97, 123, 131, 144, 148, 175
*The Family Fang* 176
*Far and Away* 8, *14-15*, 33
Farrant, Kim 13
Ferran, Pascale 76
Firth, Colin 12
Flanagan, Fionnula 101
Fleming, Victor 105
*Flirting* 7, 8, 79
Folland, Alison 33, *35*
*Forrest Gump* 171
Fosse, Bob 80, 81
Foster, Jodie 29, 171
Foucault, Michel 130
Frears, Stephen 29
*Fringe* 144
*Fur: An Imaginary Portrait of Diane Arbus* 13, 44, 136, 152, 160, 175, *178*
Garbo, Greta 17, 81, 92, 144
Gardner, Ava 76
Gautier, Eric 155

Gazzara, Ben *126, 127*
Gellhorn, Martha 28, 66, 160, 176
*Genius* 176
*Gentlemen Prefer Blondes* 81
Gibson, Mel 8
*Gilda* 80, 81
Glass, Philip 113
Glazer, Jonathan 13, 44, 136, 140, 148, 175
Glen, Iain 64
*The Golden Compass* 44, 105, 148, *177*
*Gorillas in the Mist* 29
*Grace of Monaco* 13, 154, *155-6, 157-9*, 160, *161-7, 168, 169*, 176
*The Graduate* 33
Grant, Richard E. 47, *48*
Griffith, Melanie 29
*Happy Feet* 175
Hare, David 64, 109, 175
Harris, Ed 12, 109
Harvey, Laurence 19
Hawks, Howard 81
Hayes, Terry 19, 31
Hayworth, Rita 81
*Heaven Can Wait* 33
Hemingway, Ernest 28, 66, 176
*Hemingway & Gellhorn* 13, 28, 66, 160, 176
Henry, Buck 33
Hepburn, Audrey 17
Hepburn, Katharine 17, 20, 171
Hershey, Barbara 47, *52-3, 55*, 60
Herzog, Werner 7, 8, 152, 160, 176, *177*
*High Society* 155
Hirschbiegel, Oliver *12*, 13, 139, *178*
Hitchcock, Alfred 20, 95, *155-6, 158-9*, 165
Hoffman, Dustin 33
Hopper, Dennis 19
*The Hours* 13, 25, *108*, 109, *110-7*, 119-21, 123, 160, 175

Howard, Ron 8, *14-15*, 33
*The Human Stain* 8-9, 29, 119, *174*, 175
Huppert, Isabelle 152
*I Have Never Forgotten You: The Life & Legacy of Simon Wiesenthal* 12
*In the Cut* 59, 171
*In Vogue: The Editor's Eye* 12
*The Interpreter* 13, 44, 136, 175, *178*
*The Invasion* 12, 13, *139*, *178*
James, Henry 44, 47, 58
Jason Leigh, Jennifer 33
*Jaws* 20
Jenkins, Michael 8
Joffé, Rowan 13
Jolie, Angelina 105, 171
Kaplan, Jonathan 29
Kar Wai, Wong 171
Kaufman, Philip 13, 28, 66, 160, 176
Keaton, Michael 33
Kidman, Nicole
    Isabel Archer 46-61
    Becca Corbett 138-53
    Alice Harford 62-77, 85, 148
    Rae Ingram 18-31
    Grace Kelly 95, 152, 154-69, 176
    Grace Margaret Mulligan 95, 122-37, 171
    Satine 78-93, 97
    Grace Stewart 13, 94-107, 113, 156
    Suzanne Stone Maretto 32-45, 49, 97
    Virginia Woolf 13, 106, 108-21, 160, 175
King, Paul 13, 105
*Knife in the Water* 20
Kodar, Oja 19
Koman, Jacek 82-3
Kubrick, Stanley 7, 13, 59-60, 62, 63-4, 66-7, 68-9, 72-3, 75-6, 131, 144, 175
*The Lady From Shanghai* 171
Langella, Frank 156, *161*
Law, Jude 175
Le Clézio, J. M. G. 97, 101
Lecter, Hannibal 38
Leder, Mimi 8, 13, 44, 89
Leguizamo, John 82-3
Leigh, Vivien 95
Lherault, Marie 20, 25, 47
*Lolita* 60
Lombard, Carole 33
Luhrmann, Baz 7, 13, 44, 59, 79, 84, 85, 89, 92, 136, 148, *172-3*, 176
*Mad Max* 19

*Maleficent* 105
Malkovich, John 46, 47, 58
*Manderlay* 131, 136, 171
Mann, Alakina 94, 95
Mann, Thomas 47
*Margot at the Wedding* 44
Marshall, Rob 13, 44, 139, 171
Martin, Catherine 81
Maynard, Joyce 33
McDonald, Garry 82-3
McGregor, Ewan 79, 82-3, 89
Miller, George 7, 17, 19, 31, 59, 175
Minghella, Antony 8, 44, 119, 175
Montgomery, Elizabeth 60
Monroe, Marilyn 35, 81, 92
Monton, Vincent 66
Moore, Julianne 95, 109, 113
Moreau, Jeanne 19
Morin, Edgar 75, 111, 127, 149
Mortensen, Viggo 47, 49, *50*
*Moulin Rouge!* 13, 44, 76, 79, 81, 84-5, 89, 92, 95, 97, 98-9, 101, 118, 123, 175
*Mr. & Mrs. Smith* 171
*Mrs Dalloway* 109, 111
*My Life* 33
Neill, Sam 19, 22-3, 31, 175
Nichols, Mike 29
*Nine* 44, 139
Noonan, Chris 8
Novak, Kim 38
Noyce, Phillip 13, 19-20, 25, 66
O'Connell, John 79
Ophelia 20, 25, 111
Ophuls, Marcel 19
Ophuls, Max 64
Orpheus 25, 29, 85, 144
*The Others* 13, 92, 94, 95, 101, 104-6, 113, 123, 148, 156, 175
Owen, Clive 28, 66, 176
Oz, Frank 81, 136, *177*
*Paddington* 13, 105
Paltrow, Gwyneth 155
*Panic Room* 171
*The Paperboy* 12, 44, 66, 105, 176
Parker, Mary-Louise 54
Pasztor, Beatrix Aruna 35
*The Peacemaker* 8, 44, 89
Peck, Agnès 60, 81, 85, 89
Penn, Sean 175
Pfeiffer, Michelle 171
Phoenix, Joaquin 33, 35, 45, 175
*Photograph 51* 176
*The Piano* 45, 58

*Pirates* 20
Pliskin, Fabrice 38, 42
Polanski, Roman 20
Pollack, Sydney 13, 44, 136, 175, *178*
*The Portrait of a Lady* 13, 44, 47, 50, 55, 58-60, *61*, 104, 175
*Practical Magic* 8, 12, 105
Proust, Marcel 47
*Psycho* 106
Purinton, Miles 134
*Queen of the Desert* 8, 152, 160, 176, *177*
Quignard, Pascal 95
Quine, Richard 38
*Rabbit Hole* 12-13, 44, 136, 138, 139, *140-3*, 144, 145-7, 148, *149-53*, 176
*The Railway Man* 13, *16*, 44, 160
Rainier (prince) 155-6, 161, *162-3*
*The Reader* 171
*Rebecca* 95
Richardson, Miranda 112, *113*
Rimbaud, Arthur 25
Roberts, Julia 17
*Ronde (La)* 64
Rossellini, Roberto 136
Roth, Ann 12, 109, 139
Roth, Tim 155, *162-3*
Roxburgh, Richard 79
Rubin, Bruce Joel 33
Ryan, Meg 33-4, 171
Safran, Henri 8
Sautet, Claude 19
Savides, Harris 12
Scheherazade 7, 171
Schepisi, Fred 29
Schnitzler, Arthur 63-4, 76, 175
Schumacher, Joel 12-13, 33, *174*, 175
Scott, Tony 31, 33, *174*, 175
*The Second Sex* 58
Semler, Dean 20
Serres, Michel 17, 171
Sevigny, Chloë 127
Shainberg, Steven 13, 44, 136, 160, 175, *178*
Shaw, Dash 144
*The Shining* 60
Sirk, Douglas 35, 75
Skarsgård, Stellan 12, 127, 128-9, 134
*Sleepless in Seattle* 171
Smart, Pamela 33
*Somethin' Stupid* 28
*Snow White and the Huntsman* 105
Spielberg, Steven 20, 176

*The Stepford Wives* 81, 89, 136, *177*
Stewart, James 38
*Stoker* 8, *10-11*, 12, 44, 148, 177
Stone, Sharon 66, 95
*Strangerland* 13, 176
Streep, Meryl 17, 29, 44, 109, 113
*Sunset Boulevard* 38
Swanson, Gloria 38
Teller, Miles 139, *145*
Teplitzky, Jonathan 13, *16*, 44, 160
Theron, Charlize 105, 155
Thomson, David 31, 33, 58, 97, 112, 134
*To Die For* 13, 32, 33, *34-7*, 38, *39-43*, 45, 47, 49, 60, 66, 81, 89, 97, 105, 118, 144, 148, 175
Tolstoy, Leo 7
Trank, Richard 12
*Traumnovelle* 63
Trenchard-Smith, Brian 7-8
*Trespass* 12
Truffaut, François 19
*Ulysses* 25
Urban, Keith 139, 148, 176
Van Sant, Gus 7, 13, 32, 33, 42, 66, 175
*Vietnam* 8, 19, 31, 175
Von Sternberg, Josef *80*, 81
Von Trier, Lars 7, 13, 44, 59, 95, 119, 122, 123, 127, 131, 134, 136, 171, 175
Walken, Christopher 12
Wasikowska, Mia *148*
Watts, Naomi 8, 17, 175
Weaver, Sigourney 19, 29
Weitz, Chris 44, 105, 148, *177*
Welles, Orson 19, 29
West, Blake 12
Whittet, Matthew 82-3
Wiest, Dianne 12, *145*
Wilder, Billy 38
Williams, Charles 19
Williams, Robbie 28
Willis, Bruce 33
*Windrider* 66
Winslet, Kate 171
Winters, Shelley 60
Witherspoon, Reese 155
*The Wizard of Oz* 105, 148
*Women on Top: Hollywood and Power* 12
*Working Girl* 29
Wyburd, Sophie *116-17*
Zane, Billy 19, 26-7, 31
Zemeckis, Robert 171
Ziskin, Laura 33

Original title:
*Nicole Kidman*
© 2016 Cahiers du cinéma
SARL.

Titre original :
*Nicole Kidman*
© 2016 Cahiers du cinéma
SARL.

This edition published
by Phaidon Press Limited
under licence from
Cahiers du cinéma SARL,
18–20, rue Claude-Tillier,
75012 Paris, France
© 2016 Cahiers du cinéma
SARL.

Cette édition est publiée
par Phaidon Press Limited
avec l'autorisation des
Cahiers du cinéma SARL,
18-20, rue Claude-Tillier,
75012 Paris, France
© 2016 Cahiers du cinéma
SARL.

Cahiers du cinéma
18–20, rue Claude-Tillier
75012 Paris

www.cahiersducinema.com

ISBN 978 0 7148 6803 5

A CIP catalogue record
of this book is available
from the British Library.

Editor:
Amélie Despérier-Bougdira
Project Editor:
Bamiyan Shiff
for Fast for Word
Series Concept Design:
Thomas Mayfried
Layout: Pascale Coulon
Translation from the French:
Anne McDowall
Copy-Editors:
Lise Connellan, Jane Ace
Proofreader: Sonia Roe
Picture Research:
Carolina Lucibello
Reproduction: Ilc-Point 4

Printed in China

*Photographic credits*

Coll. Cahiers du cinéma, Nilsen Première : p. 6 ; Coll. Christophel © Samuel Goldwyn Films : p. 8 (left) ; Coll. Christophel © Barron Ent't : p. 8 (right) ; Coll. Christophel © Miramax, Takashi Seida : p. 9 ; Coll. Photo 12, Archives du 7ᵉ Art © Fox Searchlight Pictures, Macall Polay : pp. 10–11 ; Coll. Photo 12, Warner Bros : p. 12 ; Coll. Photo 12 © New Line Features, James Bridges : p. 13 ; Coll. Photo 12, Archives du 7ᵉ Art : pp. 14–15 ; Coll. Christophel © Archer Street Productions, Latitude Media, Lionsgate : p. 16 (top) ; Coll. Photo 12, Archives du 7ᵉ Art, Miramax ; p. 16 (bottom) ; Coll. Christophel © Kennedy Miller Productions : p. 18 ; © Kennedy Miller Productions : pp. 21, 24, 30 ; Coll. Photo 12, Archives du 7ᵉ Art © Kennedy Miller Productions : pp. 22–3, 29 ; Coll. Cahiers du cinéma © Kennedy Miller Productions : pp. 26–7 ; Coll. Cahiers du cinéma © HBO : p. 28 ; Coll. Cahiers du cinéma © Columbia Pictures : pp. 32, 40–1 ; © Columbia Pictures : pp. 34, 39, 42, 178 (top left) ; Coll. Cahiers du cinéma © Columbia Pictures : pp. 35, 36–7 ; Coll. Photo 12 © Columbia Pictures : p. 43 ; Coll. Photo 12 © New Line Features : p. 44 ; Coll. Photo 12, Archives du 7ᵉ Art © Columbia Pictures : p. 45 ; Coll. Christophel © Polygram Film Productions : p. 46 ; © Polygram Film Productions : pp. 48–9, 50, 54–5, 58 ; Coll. Photo 12, Archives du 7ᵉ Art © Polygram Film Productions : pp. 51–3 ; Coll. Christophel © Polygram Film Productions : pp. 56–7 ; © Theodore Wood, Camerapress, Gamma : p. 59 ; Coll. Photo 12, Archives du 7ᵉ Art © Polygram Film Productions : p. 61 ; Coll. Cahiers du cinéma © Warner Bros : pp. 62, 77 ; © Warner Bros : pp. 64, 65, 67, 70–1, 74–5, 178 (bottom right) ; Coll. Cahiers du cinéma © Millennium Films : p. 66 ; Coll. Cahiers du cinéma, Manuel Harlan © Warner Bros : pp. 68–9, 72–3 ; Coll. Cahiers du cinéma © Twentieth Century Fox : p. 78 ; © Twentieth Century Fox : pp. 80, 88 ; Coll. Christophel © Twentieth Century Fox : pp. 82–3, 90–1 ; © DR : p. 84 ; Coll. Cahiers du cinéma, Sue Adler © Twentieth Century Fox : p. 85 ; Coll. Cahiers du cinéma, Douglas Kirkland © Twentieth Century Fox : pp. 86–7 ; Coll. Cahiers du cinéma © Twentieth Century Fox : p. 89 ; Coll. Christophel © Twentieth Century Fox : p. 93 ; Coll. Christophel © Cruise, Wagner Productions : pp. 94, 98–9, 102–3, 107 ; Coll. Photo 12 © Cruise, Wagner Productions : pp. 96 (top), 106 ; © Cruise, Wagner Productions : pp. 96 (bottom), 97, 100, 104 ; Coll. Photo 12, Archives du 7ᵉ Art © Columbia Pictures : p. 105 ; Coll. Cahiers du cinéma © Paramount Pictures, Miramax : pp. 108, 116–7, 119, 120–1 ; © Paramount Pictures, Miramax : pp. 110–3 ; Coll. Photo 12 © Paramount Pictures, Miramax : p. 114 ; Coll. Photo 12, Archives du 7ᵉ Art © Paramount Pictures, Miramax : p. 115 ; © Nick Ut, AP, SIPA : p. 118 ; Coll. Cahiers du cinéma © Zentropa Ent't : pp. 122, 124–33, 137 © Zentropa Ent't : p. 135 ; Coll. Photo 12, Archives du 7ᵉ Art © OP EVE 2 : p. 138 ; © OP EVE 2 : pp. 140–1, 145, 152 ; Coll. Cahiers du cinéma © OP EVE 2 : pp. 142–3, 146–7, 150–1 ; Coll. Cahiers du cinéma © Fox Searchlight Pictures : p. 148 ; Coll. Cahiers du cinéma © OP EVE 2 : p. 153 ; Coll. Cahiers du cinéma © Stone Angels, Gaumont : pp. 154, 158–9, 162–3, 165, 166–7, 169 ; © Stone Angels, Gaumont : pp. 157, 161, 164 ; Coll. Cahiers du cinéma © River Road Ent't : p. 160 ; Coll. Cahiers du cinéma, Twentieth Century Fox : pp. 172–3 ; Coll. Photo 12 © Kennedy Miller Productions : p. 174 (top left) ; Coll. Photo 12, Archives du 7ᵉ Art © Paramount Pictures : p. 174 (top right) ; Coll. Christophel © Warner Bros : p. 174 (bottom right) ; Coll. Christophel © Miramax, Lakeshore Entertainment : p. 174 (bottom right) ; Coll. Christophel © Paramount Pictures, DreamWorks SKG : p. 177 (top left) ; Coll. Cahiers du cinéma © New Line Cinema : p. 177 (top right) ; Coll. Photo 12, Archives du 7ᵉ Art © Fox Searchlight Pictures : p. 177 (bottom left) ; Coll. Cahiers du cinéma © Benaroya Pictures : p. 177 (bottom right) ; © Universal Pictures : p. 178 (top right) ; © Picture House : p. 178 (bottom left) ; Coll. Photo 12, Archives du 7ᵉ Art © Miramax Films : p. 189.

*All reasonable efforts have been made to trace the copyright holders of the photographs used in this book. We apologize to anyone that we were unable to reach.*

*Cover illustration*
Nicole Kidman by Matt Sayles, 2010.